Growing Point

Alfred Heidenreich

Growing Point

The Story of the Foundation of The Christian Community

Floris Books

First published in 1965 by the Christian Community Press. This second edition revised by Michael Tapp published in 1979.

British Library Cataloguing in Publication Data

Heidenreich, Alfred
Growing point. 2nd ed.
1. Christian Community (*Founded 1922*)
I. Title
289.9

ISBN 0-903540-17-7

Printed in Great Britain
by T & A Constable Ltd, Edinburgh

Contents

Foreword

In preparing a new edition of this book only a few changes have been made to the original text. Although Alfred Heidenreich himself wrote in his introduction that no description of the foundation of The Christian Community can be a private report, it could nevertheless be claimed that in addition to providing us with historical facts he also does give a characteristic personal commentary on many fundamental issues which such a new foundation inevitably raises. The overall result, therefore, is something of a personal testimony which can really only be altered in terms of updating the historical material.

Alfred Heidenreich was born in Regensburg, the fifth of six children of a Bavarian civil servant, on January 17, 1898. In 1916 after eight and a half years traditional classical education at the ancient city grammar school — during the second half of which he was largely absorbed by his membership of the youth movement — he joined the army and for a brief while experienced life at the front. Just before the war ended he was captured and spent a year in British captivity in France. After his release the thread of the past was soon taken up again. Back in his youth movement activities and at university he met Marta Heimeran. She was soon to meet the work of Rudolf Steiner and to introduce a reluctant Alfred Heidenreich to it by 'inviting' him to one of Steiner's courses. The result was decisive. They both joined the group of people interested in ways of bringing about a Christian renewal and from the autumn of 1921 they both belonged actively to it. Heidenreich was always a leader. So too, from the

Alfred Heidenreich in 1956 shortly after writing the original articles on which Growing Point *was based.*

foundation of The Christian Community he belonged to the circle of office-holders, as lenker until 1938 and then as oberlenker* until his death during a visit to South Africa in March 1969.

After working together for seven years in Frankfurt, Alfred Heidenreich and Marta Heimeran married and moved to London. Here, in very humble circumstances, they began the work of The Christian Community in the English language. In 1939, convinced that he should remain in England in the event of war, Alfred Heidenreich arrived back from a holiday on the Continent on British soil only minutes before war was declared and he was able to work unhindered throughout the war. His wife and their son remained in Germany. After the end of the war they did not resume their life together. Marta Heimeran then worked principally in the South German university town of Tübingen until her death in 1965. Their son, Michael, entered the priesthood of The Christian Community in 1962 and was

* The Christian Community has an administrative hierarchy of office-holders known as lenker, oberlenker, and erzoberlenker, the last being the head of the Community. The oberlenkers (usually two) together with the erzoberlenker form its international leadership while the lenkers administer regions.

appointed a lenker in 1978 with special responsibilities in South-west Germany and South Africa.

After the war Alfred Heidenreich's work grew considerably. Besides the development of the Community's work in Britain he actively participated in the expansion to the States, to South America and to South Africa and he remained until his death one of the oberlenkers, from 1939 to 1959 with Emil Bock and Gottfried Husemann, and from 1959 with Rudolf Frieling and Gottfried Husemann.

But it was undoubtedly in the English speaking world that he felt his main task to be. His was possibly one of the most successful adaptions to British life that a 'foreigner' could achieve. His masterly grasp of the language and his love of the country, not excepting its country houses, were a constant source of wonder. He had a quick grasp of business and of the law and was able to put all this to good effect as the 'complete pioneer' in starting from nothing and building the Community on sure foundations. He successfully combined the idealism of his Central European background with the pragmatism of his adopted country, a rare gift which allows for the interplay between the goal sought and the means that appear for its realization. This fine balance of the spiritual and material, the ideal and the practical, was supported by a fertile and original theological mind which can be appreciated in the many articles he wrote for the Christian Community Journal, which he edited for many years and in the lectures he gave at the end of his life on the Gospels and on the Apocalypse.*

A pictorial commentary has been added to Heidenreich's original text. The pictures fall into three main categories: those concerned with Heidenreich's own life and background, those connected with the foundation of the Community and the early years in Germany, and those which document its history where he spent the greater part of his working years, Britain, together with brief excursions into America and Africa. Particular thanks are due to Michael Heidenreich for help in collecting the pictures.

Michael Tapp

* See *The Unknown in the Gospels*, Christian Community Press, 1972, and *The Book of Revelation*, Floris Books, 1977.

Introduction

This story is written chiefly for members and friends of The Christian Community who have seen this movement for religious renewal in action, and who may wish to know how it all started. It does not presume to be anything like a definitive history, but it is more like an older member of the family telling its younger members about the way in which the family began, what adventures those had who laid the foundations, what trials and difficulties they went through, and how they triumphed over adversity. But while in this sense it is an inside story, it is not a private report. Anyone interested is welcome to read it. Yet he should not expect to get to know and to understand The Christian Community *only* by reading this history of its beginnings.

If we were only told how a child is born, and never set eyes on an adult man or woman we should not know a great deal about the human being. But if we have lived to adulthood and know what a man or woman is like, we shall certainly add to our understanding if we learn about childbirth. In a similar way, if we have met The Christian Community in life, the knowledge of its origin will deepen our vision of its significance. But those for whom this book is the first contact, and who feel their interest aroused by the story, should accept our warm invitation to come and see the grown and growing creature whose birth is here described.

I am writing as an eyewitness and as one of the founders of the movement. It is in the nature of things that such a first account

In the trenches at the front line shortly before being captured, Heidenreich in the centre of the group.

should have a personal angle. For anyone who had an active share in the foundation it is difficult if not impossible to write a purely impersonal record. The heart still beats more strongly at the memory of these events, and the blood courses quicker through veins and arteries. I shall venture, therefore, to begin with a personal introduction.

The scene is Germany, October 1919. I had just been released as prisoner of war. I had been taken by the British in October 1918, a month before the Armistice, right on the famous Ypres road, half-way between Ypres and Menin. For a full year my type of prisoner had been kept in open-air wire cages under British administration on French soil. Most of the time the conditions had been appalling. But now I was back and free and life could begin again.

The collapse of the old Germany did not worry me much. I had seen it come even as a schoolboy, and still more clearly in the army. Now I had to find a place in the new order of things. On paper I was an enrolled University student and had already a few terms to my credit, a privilege given to serving soldiers and prisoners of war. It was the natural and logical step now to become a student in reality. I began reading economics in

Munich. After the winter term I took my bicycle and, with all my belongings in a rucksack, I rode 600 miles across Germany to the Baltic and enrolled as a law student at the University of Rostock for the summer. In the following winter I was back in the south reading history, having tasted the universities of Berlin and Breslau as a guest student on the way. The next summer term I found myself studying languages at Tübingen.

What was I doing? Was it the after-effects of war and imprisonment that made it difficult for me to settle? For a long time I thought this was so, and that the fault lay with me. But gradually I sensed that my profound disappointment with university life had another cause. I had accepted the universities unquestioningly as the sources of learning which offered the key to the mastery of life. But I became aware that this had been an illusion. It might be that the universities still held the key to jobs in the Establishment. But had not the Establishment miserably and ignominiously collapsed all round? Instinctively I realized that the traditional academic approach to the world had a great deal to do with the 'decline of the West', of which it was fashionable to speak. It dawned on me that the German universities — 'the intellectual body-guard of the Hohenzollern' as they had proudly called themselves — were in a large measure the intellectual fathers of a way of life which had been discredited by the verdict of history. I could not have put it so bluntly or precisely at the time. But at bottom this is what I felt and this was the cause of my malaise.

In this condition I met Rudolf Steiner. It was at the beginning of the first conference for university students which he conducted in Germany. He had held one such conference before at the opening of the Goetheanum, his School for Spiritual Science, near Basle in October 1920. Now in February 1921 he held the first of these conferences in Germany, in Stuttgart.

I took part in every session. I understood little of what Steiner said. But after a week I knew I had found my university; and after a fortnight I took a number of friends with me to him for a personal interview. From that moment none of us ever turned back.

Looking back today over nearly half a century, I can only testify that Steiner and his work has fulfilled a hundred times and more the unspoken promise of that first encounter. Of course now his fame is spreading apace. Steiner schools where his

Heidenreich as a young man.

philosophy of education is applied have been founded in many countries; homes and settlements for the mentally and physically handicapped have been set up all over the world, where his deep insight into the psychosomatic facts of human nature is a constant guide and inspiration for the care of these unfortunate brothers and sisters of us all. Steiner hospitals and nursing homes, centres for speech and drama, art schools, centres for the study of industrial relations, schools of eurythmy, centres for adult education and a variety of other foundations bear witness today to the universality of his creative genius

I have had the good fortune in the course of my activities to see a fair portion of the globe, and to read a good deal in the process. But wherever I went it was Steiner to whom I would finally turn in my mind. He was the best guide. Steiner's lectures helped me to understand the complicated social structure of the United States and the intriguing geographical mysteries of South America. His writings threw a clearer light on the antiquities of the Holy Land than any handbook. His reading of human evolution explained the oceanic destiny of Britain, the European melting pot of nations, the racial tensions of Africa. He always offered an independent spiritual point of reference.

On my journeys I have also had the privilege of meeting other great men — Gandhi, Albert Schweitzer, Archbishop Temple. Steiner was and remained in a class by himself. There simply wasn't anybody one could compare him with. He was truly extraordinary. Quiet, humble, dignified, immensely alert, he touched every subject with the unassuming assurance of a master and the originality of genius. In a word: in him the evolution of human consciousness had reached a new stage. While we ordinary mortals sit in the Platonic cave with our backs to reality painfully deciphering the shadows cast against the inner wall, Steiner achieved the spiritual feat of turning round. Eventually he saw reality face to face.

It was with and through and by the help and advice of Rudolf Steiner that the movement came into being whose first beginnings are now to be related.

1 Roots

In the early months of 1917 Rudolf Steiner gave a series of lectures in Berlin. In the third of these lectures he touched on the mystery of the Holy Trinity and in this context he made a somewhat unusual aside.

> At this stage I believe I ought to make a statement which is important and which should be well understood by the friends of Spiritual Science.* It should not be represented that spiritual-scientific endeavours are intended as a substitute for the life and practice of religion. Spiritual Science can in the highest degree, and particularly concerning the Mystery of Christ, be taken as a support, as a foundation for the life and practice of religion. But Spiritual Science should not be made into a religion. It ought to be clear that religion in its vital life, its living practice within the human community enkindles the spirit-consciousness of the soul. If this spirit-consciousness is to be quickened within the human being, he cannot stop short at abstract ideas of God or Christ, but must ever anew be engaged in religious practices and activities, which in different people may take different forms; he must live in a religious atmosphere, in a religious milieu which speaks to him.†

Rudolf Steiner proceeded then to say that the spirit-consciousness which is attained in a living religious practice can lead to the desire for more detailed spiritual knowledge, which in turn becomes a further objective support for the religious life.

This was a telling statement. Steiner felt a deep concern for

* 'Spiritual Science' is the phrase normally adopted in translation for Steiner's *Geisteswissenschaft*. For the sake of conformity with other publications I have generally retained this phrase. But on occasion I have used 'Science of Spirit' which I believe to be a more adequate rendering of the German term.

† *Kosmische und menschliche Metamorphose*, February 20, 1917. (*Cosmic and Human Metamorphoses*, Anthroposophical Publ. Co., London 1926.)

certain developments at the time. In order to understand the significance of this, a short glance into earlier years is necessary. When, after a distinguished career as editor of Goethe's scientific works, and as editor of a leading weekly magazine in Berlin, Steiner began at the turn of the century to concentrate on his esoteric studies and occult research, he found a first following among the members of the Theosophical Society. For about ten years it was within the framework of the Theosophical Society that his own Anthroposophical Society took shape. In 1912 the break came. Steiner had recognized in Christ the unique cosmic saviour, the Son of God born in eternity. The Theosophical Society regarded Christ as one of the many spiritual guides of mankind. When Annie Besant founded the movement of the 'Star of the East', and proclaimed Krishnamurti as the incarnation of Christ in our time, the breach was complete and absolute.

In the building up of his Anthroposophical Movement within the Theosophical Society Rudolf Steiner had given great care and prominence to the teaching of Christocentric truths. This was also in accordance with the request of the members. Writing of this period in his autobiography Steiner says: 'There was in the first place a strong desire to hear a presentation of the Gospels and of the Bible in general in the light of Anthroposophy. There was a wish to hear in a series of studies about these relevations which had been given to mankind.'

These early series of studies, or 'cycles' as they were generally called, were intimate events. The membership was small, single-minded and devoted. Few of these first disciples had maintained any connections with a church. The meetings in which the unique personality of Rudolf Steiner himself spoke to them out of the spirit about the great spiritual documents of Christianity provided all the religious life they needed.

But matters changed when the war broke out in 1914 and changed increasingly as the war proceeded. Other problems presented themselves. The world itself knocked at the door. Steiner took up the challenge. The comparative seclusion of earlier years had to give way to increasing public activity. Steiner began to speak to the burning topics of the day. A new type of listener came to his meetings; numbers grew. Now his lectures could no longer take the place of religion. It would not do if the newcomers mistook his activities or if it were 'represented that spiritual-scientific endeavours are intended as a substitute for the life and practice of religion'. And so he felt compelled to utter a serious warning. Whoever cares to look up his warning in its original context, cannot fail to sense the earnestness and emphasis with which he uttered it. He clearly went out of his way to do so.

It is difficult to say whether the implications of this statement were fully appreciated by many of those who listened to that lecture. But it struck home with some young people who, rather like myself, had begun to look to Steiner as a leader. It so happened that among them were also some students of theology. Among themselves they had begun to wonder whether theology had any future at all, or whether the churches had had their day and something else should take their place. Now, of course, they pricked up their ears. One of them could even report a remark made by Rudolf Steiner in a private conversation to another student of theology, that 'immeasurable benefit could be derived for humanity, if a number of young men would seize the pulpits'. What did he mean? Was there a task to be taken up, a duty to perform? Was there a fresh opening for bringing the fruits of the Science of Spirit to greater numbers? Was there a new sphere waiting for the active application of this Science? Were there others who would come forward? How could one find out?

There is a tide in the affairs of men. It flowed strongly in the spring of 1921. The students' conference mentioned above had been so successful, that Steiner followed it up with another series of lectures in Stuttgart on 'Science and the historic development of humanity since the time of antiquity'. Again students from a number of universities came to Stuttgart to hear him.

One day some of them talking together discovered that they had the same question on their minds. In a little café one of them produced a cyclostyled copy of the shorthand transcript which had been made of the series of lectures in Berlin *Cosmic and Human Metamorphoses*. He read out the passage quoted above. The spark flashed and set minds ablaze. It was decided there and then to approach Steiner with a short memorandum. Only he could answer the question and his answer would be decisive and final. Inspired and guided by that provoking passage they drew up the following document which was presented to Rudolf Steiner the same evening.

We, the undersigned, are convinced that the unfolding of spirit-consciousness is what humanity today is wanting above all to achieve; and we are convinced moreover that 'religion in its vital life, in its living practice within the social life enkindles spirit-consciousness'. These two facts seem to us to indicate a direction for the activity that we have perhaps to undertake from within the anthroposophical movement.

We are only able in this present time to approach the idea of priesthood — priesthood as connected with the practice of religion — with a certain caution and reserve, so long as on the one hand it is derived only from such priestly and clerical institutions as have existed hitherto; and inasmuch as on the other hand we do not know whether something like priesthood has to be at all, or whether something else must be put in its place. Finally it is our belief that all further questions concerning what has been described as religious practice and religious activity, or concerning the religious milieu that ought to form the environment of man's life from birth to death, can only rightly be put when his first question has been dealt with. We therefore now ask Dr Steiner to give us information on this matter.

From the answer, each one of us will see for himself whether he is able to undertake a task in this connection or not.

Stuttgart, May 22, 1921.

[Signed by some twenty students]

This document, in which the historian will not fail to recognize the great reserve and respect with which these young people approached Rudolf Steiner, was the first formulated initiative towards that which in due course was born as The Christian Community.

Rudolf Steiner responded at once. He invited the two representatives who had handed him the letter to an interview. Notes of this interview exist, written out by one of the two. Rudolf Steiner made sure of the sincerity and strength of their impulse, and being satisfied, promised an early meeting of several days, with lectures and discussions in which he would explain what should be done. 'About all these matters one must speak at length,' he said. The promised meeting, which took

Da nach unserer Überzeugung die Entfaltung des Geistbewußtseins dasjenige ist, was die gegenwärtige Menschheit zunächst erwerben will und da außerdem „Religion in ihrem lebendigen Leben, in ihrem lebendigen Geübtwerden innerhalb der menschlichen Gesellschaft das Geistbewußtsein entfacht", sehen die unterzeichneten Studenten aus diesen Tatsachen eine Richtung sich ergeben für die Tätigkeit, die sie aus der anthroposophischen Bewegung heraus vielleicht auszuüben haben.

Da wir an den heute mit der Ausübung der Religion verbundenen Begriff des Priestertums nur mit einer gewissen Scheu herangehen können, solange einerseits derselbe nur abgeleitet wird von dem, was bis heute als priesterliche oder kirchliche Institution dagewesen ist und da wir andererseits nicht wissen, ob überhaupt etwas ähnliches oder wie etwas anderes an dessen Stelle treten muß; da wir schließlich glauben, daß alle weiteren Fragen nach dem, was mit religiöser Übung und religiöser Betätigung umschrieben würde und nach dem, was als religiöses Milieu das menschliche Leben von der Geburt bis zum Tode zu umgeben habe, erst richtig gestellt werden können, nachdem auf diese erste Frage eingegangen worden ist, bitten wir Herrn Dr. Steiner von Herzen, uns über diese Frage Auskunft zu geben.

Aus einer Antwort kann sich für den einzelnen ergeben, ob er in diesem Zusammenhang Aufgaben zu erfüllen im Stande ist.

Stuttgart, den 22. Mai 1921

Werner Klein, stud. philos.
Gertrud Spörri, stud. theol.
Ludwig Köhler. stud. theol.
Gottfried Husemann, stud. chem. früher theol.

Bitte wenden!

In demselben Sinne haben eine Erklärung abgegeben:

Robert Spörri, cand. theol. Zürich
Wilhelm Clormann, cand theol. Mannheim
Ludwig Nonnenmacher, stud. theol. Mannheim
Walter Gradenwitz, stud. theol. Wiesbaden
Martin Borchart, stud. phil. et theol. Marburg
Rudolf Meyer, Hamburg
Richard Gitzke, stud. theol. Berlin
Otto Franke, stud. theol. Berlin
Horst Münzer, stud. phil. et theol. Berlin
Emil Bock, cand. theol. Charlottenburg
Eberhard Kurras, cand. theol. Saaleck (Thüring.)
Ernst Umlauff, stud. philos. Breslau
Otto Becker, Hauslehrer, Holzminden

Es fehlen noch einige Unterschriften.

The document presented to Steiner.

place from June 12 to 16, 1921, grew to the size of a full course. From the beginning it far, far surpassed all expectations. Rudolf Steiner revealed his power from a new angle. He showed himself as a complete master of all things which belong to the life of a church. Ritual, priesthood, pastoral care, organization and finance, social tasks and responsibilities, everything was touched upon with unmatched originality and fullness. Many revolutionary points were put forward with complete matter of factness. The movement should form free congregations, women were to work on a basis of complete equality with men, the sacramental mysteries of Christianity were to be renewed.

It will for ever be difficult to convey the quality of such meetings with Rudolf Steiner. Even the greatest parallels break down. The most astounding feature was the concentration and single-mindedness with which Rudolf Steiner conducted such meetings. He gave the impression as if the subject in hand were his one and only object in life, as if he had never done anything else. And yet one knew that on the same day he would conduct probably two or three other meetings, on entirely different subjects, with the same application and mastery.

As the next step Rudolf Steiner proposed a comprehensive course in the following autumn. He regarded it as essential, however, that the numbers should by then be ten times bigger than the original twenty who had signed the memorandum. The target had not been fully reached when the time came, but Rudolf Steiner, who was always ready to meet honest endeavour half-way, expressed himself content with the number of about 120 who assembled at the Goetheanum in September 1921.

Steiner began the course on an advanced level. But the composition of the audience was less homogeneous than it had been in the spring. In the endeavour to reach the required number, people had been invited whose unconditional preparedness was not equal to that of the original group. In particular, a number of ministers were admitted whose interest stopped short at a theological discussion. This presented a difficulty. Rudolf Steiner did not hold back his views on the future of the traditional churches. 'A hundred years from now there will be no Christian Churches left,' he said one day, 'unless something is founded like that which is intended here.' But as usual he adapted what he said and how he said it to the souls of those before him. And it soon became noticeable that he did not always keep to the same level on which he had given the first lead, but spoke more to the condition of those present.

There is, of course, no saying what might have happened if the same quality of resolve had been maintained as in the spring. But in retrospect all these historic events appear in their necessity. Once more the traditional forces had a chance of meeting with the herald of the new Christian era. Leading Protestant ministers, as well as bearers of the Apostolic succession, were among us. The outstanding figure was Dr Christian Geyer who, although he eventually felt too old to join the new movement, spoke of Rudolf Steiner as one in whom 'a whole university was present in one man'. For the younger people, to whom much of the theological discussion appeared as a waste of time, it was of great value once to have made contact in this way with the theological mind of the past, and to have witnessed Rudolf Steiner's supreme mastery in answering even abstract and theoretical questions with the word of life. For this is what he did. To this day, and for generations to come, the notes of those memorable lectures and discussions, held twice a day for more than a fortnight, are a treasure of wisdom and guidance. In the midst of the husks of the past, the growth of new life asserted itself, and the wise gardener tended it lovingly and nourished it with lasting substance.

After this course something like a hiatus occurred. Most of the fellow-travellers dropped away and the young generation was occupied with the digestion of much spiritual material which was new. In those weeks and months Rudolf Steiner stood by. He did not take any initiative; he never did in matters in which initiative had to come from others. But when a move was made to recapture the original impetus he was again immediately ready to give practical advice. And he dropped more than one hint that in his judgment the time for action was at hand.

During this winter 1921–1922 an event of supreme importance put the whole enterprise on a safe basis. Dr Friedrich Rittelmeyer resolved to throw in his lot with the new movement. I cannot do better than quote Rudolf Steiner himself, who wrote about this event two years later.

> In Dr Rittelmeyer a personality existed who in the truest meaning of the word was a Christian priest and an anthroposophist. He had, indeed, without ritual, but in a wide range of spiritual activity represented in life the Christian renewal through the working of his personality. To present something out of the Anthroposophical Society for the renewal of Christianity raised as a matter of course the practical question: How will Rittelmeyer accept what can be given? What attitude will he take towards the realization of what is intended? For the anthroposophical movement could not but see in Rittelmeyer the example of a personality who had united Christianity and Anthroposophy in the inward harmony of his heart and in the outward harmony of his work. And Rittelmeyer said 'yes!' with all his heart. Thereby a firm starting point was gained for the independent movement for Christian renewal.*

* *Mitteilungen der allgemeinen anthroposophischen Gesellschaft*, October 5, 1924.

Who was Friedrich Rittelmeyer? To the English-speaking world he was first introduced by two of his works which the Macmillan Company of New York published in 1930 and 1931.

Friedrich Rittelmeyer (1872–1938), first head of The Christian Community.

Closely associated as preachers and friends in the Lutheran Church in Nürnberg, Geyer and Rittelmeyer drew a great following. Geyer came close to joining Rittelmeyer in entering The Christian Community.

The first was his life of Jesus which appeared under the title *Behold the Man*. It was translated by two professors of the University of Pittsburgh, Erich Hofacker and George Bennett Hatfield. The second publication was *The Lord's Prayer*, translated by S. M. K. Gandell, for many years the leader of the anthroposophical group in Chicago. Of Rittelmeyer's later works his volume of letters on the guidance of the inner life, entitled *Meditation*, has become the best selling of his books in English. A frank and penetrating account of his personal meetings with Steiner, *Rudolf Steiner Enters my Life* has also run into several editions. Among the smaller books is a slender volume, *Reincarnation*, published in English in 1936.

In order to understand the importance of Friedrich Rittelmeyer for the foundation of The Christian Community, something must be known of his public position at the time. It is no exaggeration to say that at the beginning of the century Dr Rittelmeyer, together with his friend and colleague Christian Geyer (who was mentioned above), had revolutionized the art of the pulpit in Germany. It is true, this *neue Predigtmethode* did not meet with the unqualified approval of the conservative and the orthodox. Bishop Dibelius of Berlin wrote somewhat sarcastically in his memoirs: 'Rittelmeyer poured out each time a veritable cornucopia of modern literary references and brilliant thoughts over his congregation, and let it always be understood that he was intimately familiar with the problems of modern science and art.' Nevertheless, he lifted religious speaking out of the rut and the easy method of talking only to the converted.

Although Rittelmeyer held, to start with, a comparatively minor position in the established Lutheran Church of Germany, his collected sermons were read far and wide. The great Harnack read them regularly to his family, and in later years the Prussian Minister of Culture had a selection of them republished on his own initiative. In 1911, at the time when Rittelmeyer met Steiner, he had a far greater following in Germany than Steiner. Rittelmeyer could fill not only the biggest churches, but the biggest lecture halls. His followers numbered thousands, while in those days Rudolf Steiner's following numbered barely hundreds. It is to Rittelmeyer's lasting honour that he recognized, in spite of external appearances, the unique greatness of Rudolf Steiner's spiritual stature. In *Rudolf Steiner Enters my Life* he has described his first interview with Steiner, but he has not published the more intimate remarks which Rudolf Steiner himself made about this historic meeting, and perhaps the time has not yet come when others would have the right to say what Rittelmeyer himself chose to withhold.

Early in 1917 Rittelmeyer was called to Berlin, to one of the most influential pulpits in Germany, comparable perhaps to the pulpit of St. Paul's or the City Temple in London. Of his experience in this position during the last two years of the First World War, when he saw the final collapse of Imperial Germany at very close quarters, he spoke with many vivid details in his autobiography.* By the end of the war he had gained international reputation. Archbishop Soederblom of Sweden invited him to visit the Scandinavian churches. As a member of the German section of the Ecumenical Council Rittelmeyer was chosen to meet the group of leading Quakers who were the first Christian representatives of Britain to extend a handshake of peace to the Germans, and to welcome the first delegation of American bishops. It seemed then only a matter of time until Rittelmeyer would be offered the highest position in the hierarchy of the Lutheran Church in Germany.

However, events took a different turn. Rittelmeyer was in his forty-ninth year, when the turning point of his life came. Providence offered a helping hand, but did not force the issue. In 1918 he had met with an accident, in which he broke a leg, but which was not otherwise considered serious at the time. Delayed after-effects of some internal injuries compelled him, however, to go on sick-leave in the summer of 1920, and to retire from public life for nearly a year. On his sick-bed he prepared the greatest public tribute to Steiner that had yet appeared. He prevailed upon a number of leading men in various walks of life who by that time had been earnest students of Rudolf Steiner's work, to say in the form of a comprehensive article what they owed to him in the field in which they were masters. Rittelmeyer edited these collected essays and himself contributed one called 'Rudolf Steiner's Personality and Work' and one called 'Rudolf Steiner and the German Spirit', the latter a deliberate challenge to the resurgence of militant nationalism. The work appeared as a birthday gift for Rudolf Steiner's sixtieth birthday in 1921. It was the first substantial tribute to him published by an 'outside' publisher. It was a great challenge to the German intelligentsia at the time. Rittelmeyer published later in his autobiography one or

* *Aus meinem Leben*, Verlag Urachhaus, Stuttgart, 1937.

two characteristic letters which he received at the time from leaders of contemporary thought, charming and pathetic in their non-comprehension.

During this period of enforced physical inactivity Rittelmeyer found time to ponder in detachment over the proposed movement for religious renewal of which he had been kept informed from the beginning. What went on in his mind in those months was decisive. When he had sufficiently recovered to meet us, his mind was made up.

I remember very well his first appearance in our circle in Berlin in the late autumn of 1921. I must confess that for me it was something of a shock. Of course I was deeply interested and in a very real sense already committed to this coming movement for religious renewal. But anything even faintly parsonic or reminiscent of religion in the usual style sent cold shivers down my spine. It was inevitable that at that first meeting with us Rittelmeyer should still show something of the exterior of the Lutheran parson. Later on he transformed this in the most exemplary and moving manner. But for the moment some of us had to swallow hard. It was all part of the historic process.

In the following spring of 1922 during another of these conferences for university students, we had a decisive meeting with Rudolf Steiner in one of the vestries of Rittelmeyer's church in Berlin. Steiner strongly encouraged those among us who wanted now to go ahead. Soon after, Rittelmeyer offered his resignation from his position in the Lutheran Church. As a matter of fact, his letter of resignation was not even acknowledged. The ecclesiastic authorities did not write a single line of thanks or regret to the man who had given the church a quarter of a century of historic service. In the summer of that year, Rittelmeyer, Geyer and Bock, who were expected to become the leaders of the movement, were invited by Steiner to spend some time with him in Dornach for top level conversations. In these talks, which continued for several weeks, the principles of leadership in a modern Christian community were clarified.

Eventually, at long last, in the second half of August, a much sifted and reduced group gathered for a final retreat in the little village of Breitbrunn, twenty miles west of Munich, on the shores of the Ammersee at the foot of the Bavarian Alps. One of the true saints of the anthroposophical movement lived at Breitbrunn, Michael Bauer, who was one of the most intimate

View of the Ammersee at Breitbrunn.

disciples of Rudolf Steiner and an intimate friend of the poet Christian Morgenstern. He lived now in retirement. Frau Margarete Morgenstern, the widow of the poet, took care of him. He spoke very little, but it was an experience to see him walk through his little orchard. He seemed a personal friend of all his trees which confided in him and communed with him. One day he made a remark which is indelibly impressed on my mind: 'Christ is the homeliest word in the world, blessed is he who understands this.' Frau Morgenstern and he, as far as his strength allowed, had made the preparations for our stay. I shall have to say more about this in the next chapter, when I shall endeavour to present some of the personalities of the founders. For the moment it will suffice to note that even at this last moment, before the final step was to be taken at Dornach, the hand of the Potter continued to fashion this first community. Dr Geyer dropped out, and so did one or two others. On September 5 the final number of forty-five founders crossed the lake at sunrise in little boats to catch the early train which would bring them to Dornach. It was a crossing of the Rubicon.

At Dornach the difference from the year before could hardly be exaggerated. Nothing tentative or theoretical was left. From

the first moment Rudolf Steiner took everything into his own hands, and the foundation events proceeded apace. At the first meeting he told us that we should all leave Dornach different men from what we were when we came, and that we should all be ordained. He gave the name 'The Christian Community' [*Die Christengemeinschaft*] to the new Movement. 'The name must be simple and challenging,' he said. He also gave the name to the new Communion Service: 'The Act of Consecration of Man' [*Die Menschenweihehandlung*]. All this was given with the greatest naturalness in a few sentences.

During the preceding twelve months when we had struggled on the physical plane to fashion the body which should be the bearer of a new dispensation, something must have happened also in the spiritual world. Rudolf Steiner spoke of the courage

The founding priests gathered at Breitbrunn in August 1922. (Those not named were not ordained.)

1. Johannes Perthel (1888-1944); 2. Hermann Beckh (1875-1937); 3. Wolfgang Schickler (1894-1960); 4. Adolf Müller (1895-1967); 5. Wilhelm Kelber (1901-67); 6. Carl Stegmann (b. 1897); 7. Marta Heimeran (1895-1965); 8. Martin Borchart (1894-1971); 9. Friedrich Doldinger (1897-1973); 10. Rudolf Frieling (b. 1901); 11. Waldemaar Mickisch (1900-44); 12. Kurt Willmann (b. 1902); 13. Kurt Philippi (1892-1955); 14. August Pauli (1869-1959); 15. Eberhard Kurras (b. 1897); 16. Hermann Fackler (1886-1978); 17. Wilhelm Ruhtenberg (1888-1954); 18. Heinrich Ogilvie (b. 1893); 19. Alfred Heidenreich (1898-1969); 20. Rudolf von Koschützki (1866-1954); 21. Arnold Goebel (1897-1972); 22. Fritz Blattmann (1882-1969); Joachim Sydow (1899-1949); 24. Jutta Frentzel (b. 1901); 25. Gertrud Spörri (1894-1968); 26. Heinrich Rittelmeyer (1879-1960); 27. Rudolf Köhler (b. 1899); 28. Karl Ludwig (ordained in 1923, 1892-1931); 29. Otto Becher (1891-1954); 30. Gottfried Husemann (1900-72); 31. Friedrich Rittelmeyer (1872-1938); 32. Claus von der Decken (1888-1977); 33. Wilhelm Salewski (1889-1950); 34. Ludwig Koehler (b. 1900); 35. Harald Schilling (1902-43); 36. Eduard Lenz (1901-45); 37. Gerhard Klein (b. 1902); 38. Rudolf Meyer (ordained later in 1922, b. 1896); 39. Kurt von Wistinghausen (b. 1901); 40. Richard Gitzke (b. 1896); 41. Otto Franke (1897-1956); 42. Johannes Werner Klein (b. 1898); 43. Walter Gradenwitz (1898-1960); 44. Emil Bock (1895-1959); 45. Thomas Kändler (1901-57); 46. Erwin Lang (b. 1897); 47. Hermann Groh (1894-1957).

which he had himself to summon in order to approach the spiritual world for the birth of the new sacraments, but he spoke now among us as one having authority. The spiritual events followed each other in swift succession. A vow was taken, and the community of the founder circle established. Under Rudolf Steiner's close personal guidance a body of seven office holders was established. Now the preparations went ahead for the first celebration of the Act of Consecration of Man. Rudolf Steiner repeatedly read and demonstrated every detail. He gave the patterns for the priestly vestments, and the three members of the founder circle who were to become the first women priests in Christian history, took the making of them in hand. While I am writing I have before me a photograph of the carved rostrum which was transformed into the first altar. Rudolf Steiner himself carried under his arm the seven-branched candlestick, which he had brought all the way to the Goetheanum from his house. The time of actual beginning was delayed, or rather decided, by events beyond our control. Rittelmeyer was taken ill with one of those paralysing bouts of headache which as a result of his accident attacked him from time to time until the end of his life. And when he had recovered and was ready, suddenly a gust of wind lifted the heavy skylight above our heads out of its place, and laid it down athwart the opening in a dangerous position. Workmen had to be fetched, and only after they had put the heavy window securely back in its place could we begin. It was a puzzling occurrence. I remember Rudolf Steiner absorbed in close attention. It was like a pentecostal symbol projected into the physical realm, to stab us awake for what was to come.

During the first Act of Consecration of Man which now began and which proceeded in stages through several days, Friedrich Rittelmeyer received his ordination through Rudolf Steiner. He thus became the first Christian priest in the new dispensation. Through Rittelmeyer the ordination was then enacted and passed on to the rest of us.

For those who remembered what some churches teach about the so-called Apostolic succession, the event was astounding. But the reality was as plain as a sunrise. You do not dispute the sun. You bow to its rays. It has been our privilege to observe the grace and power of the renewed sacrament growing daily for nearly half a century. And have not the thousands of men and women who have since worshipped in this sacrament all over the world also seen that the hand of God has been in it from the beginning, and ever more?

On September 16, 1922 the first celebration of the Act of Consecration of Man was completed and we have since counted this day as the birthday of The Christian Community. In retrospect Rudolf Steiner himself wrote of these events:

> At the end of September and beginning of October [1921], there assembled at the Goetheanum a number of German theological students who bore in their hearts the impulse for a religious renewal in the Christian sense. The work that was begun then found its fulfilment in September 1922. The hours spent in September 1922, with these students, in the small hall of the south wing — the very spot where later the fire was first discovered [The Goetheanum was burned down in the New Year's Night 1922–1923.] — were for me an experience that I cannot but reckon as one of the solemn festivals of my life. There, in company with a group of men and women fired with a noble enthusiasm it was possible to enter on the path that carries the knowledge of the spirit into religious experience.*

For once a historic comparison may be permissible by which I have tried in after-years to understand these enormous facts, and which I offer with great reserve and respect. During the critical forty years in the wilderness, when the small fragments of the Hebrew nation were forged into the bearer of a divine promise for all mankind, Moses, the man of God, brought down from the heights of Mount Sinai the word of God for God's purpose at the time. In this process Moses was guided to establish the Levitical priesthood. But Moses did not himself assume the priestly office and function. He ordained his brother Aaron as the fountain-head of the new priesthood. Had we witnessed and were we involved in a similar event in our time? To the pedestrian mentality such a suggestion borders on madness. And indeed, the setting for the new event, the scenery and all the appearances, were as different as the coat and trousers of 1922 were from the flowing robes of the ancient Hebrews. Yet was not the difference only in the shell? Was the essential core so different? Were we not in the presence of a new Moses and a new Aaron who did exactly the same in the context of their time as those venerable figures had done in the wilderness of Sinai? The one a man of God with

* *Das Goetheanum*, Vol. II, p. 32.

a unique message who did, however, not assume the priestly office; the other his brother in the spirit who became the first priest of a new dispensation?

An initiate who will once look back from a distant future upon the history of our planet will behold in the events of September 1922 one of the crucial steps in the development of Christianity on earth since the mystery of Golgotha. Among those who took part in it, perhaps some of the older and more mature souls grasped something of the significance there and then. For most of the younger ones the events passed far beyond their conscious comprehension. It was for them more like a dream full of powerful portents and potent promise, in the gradual realization and working out of which they have spent their life to this day.

During the remaining week of this foundation meeting, the Act of Consecration of Man was celebrated every morning, so that it took place seven times within the walls of the first Goetheanum before being celebrated in the world every day, as it has been since. It so happened that I was one of the seven who was privileged to celebrate his first Act of Consecration in the first Goetheanum. The memory of this event lives within me like that of a clear spring morning.

By the end of September most of the founders returned to their various towns in Germany, where groups of interested enquirers had been previously collected. On the first Sunday in Advent 1922 the Act of Consecration of Man was celebrated in a number of towns for the first time in public. Now the Community had to make its way. Rudolf Steiner remained its unfailing 'adviser and helper'. This is how he himself described his relationship to The Christian Community. In a sense the foundation process continued as long as he lived. The prayers for the various seasons of the year, which Rudolf Steiner himself always called 'Epistles', were given through him in the course of 1923, also some further sacramental rituals. When he gave us the Burial Service for Children, he was so moved by its beauty that he had tears in his eyes. He was always accessible for innumerable questions which arose in connection with our first steps of practical experience, and in July 1923 the whole circle was again assembled with him when he gave, among other things, an example of how to translate the Greek New Testament. After the foundation of the General Anthroposophical Society at Christmas 1923, the whole relationship of The Christian Community to the Goetheanum was to be put on a new basis. In September 1924 he gave the priests' course on the Apocalypse, and he did his best to inaugurate co-operation between anthroposophical doctors and the priests of The Christian Community by a course on pastoral medicine, to which both doctors and priests were invited.

The closing phase of the foundation was to have been the appointment and induction of a supreme head of the Community, for the office of which Rudolf Steiner gave the name 'erzoberlenker'. Rudolf Steiner had promised to carry out that spiritual act himself. Alas, his final illness prevented him. He sent word not to wait any longer, and a few days before his last birthday, in February 1925, the ritual for which he had sent the text was carried out in Berlin, in the presence of Frau Marie Steiner and Dr Günther Wachsmuth, whom Rudolf Steiner had sent as his official representatives. Through this act Dr Rittelmeyer was created the first erzoberlenker of The Christian Community. Five weeks later Rudolf Steiner passed into the spiritual world.

2 Personalities of the Foundation

If a professional selection board had had to choose the personalities of the founders, I doubt that more than half a dozen of us would have been judged suitable. But a celestial selection board, or whoever they are who attend to these matters on behalf of Providence, seemed to have decided that they could somehow make do with us. We were the oddest collection of people. When a dear lady heard the peals of laughter coming from one of our meetings, she observed testily, 'Anything more unlike a Christian community . . .'

To start with, we were very unevenly divided in ages. Thirty-three of our number had not yet crossed the threshold of the twenty-eighth year; not more than three were over forty-five. Only one had already white hair, and was therefore called *Schimmel* (white horse). He was Rudolf von Koschützki, who belonged to an old aristocratic family from the eastern borders of Germany and had reached the ripe age of fifty-six. He had started life as a farmer, until a railway accident put an end to his farming career. He turned his love and knowledge of farming into writing, and produced a textbook on agriculture in three volumes which was widely used. When I visited him not long before his eighty-fifth birthday in 1951 he was busy revising the latest edition for publication. During the First World War he was chief war correspondent on the Eastern Front. He was really a distinguished writer who had moved 'from the plough to the pen', as the title of one of his books expresses it. For thirty years he served among us as a priest in Breslau, in Berlin and in

Rudolf von Koschützki (1866–1954), the oldest of the founding group had started life as a farmer.

August Pauli (1869–1959), the oldest of a number who had been Lutheran ministers.

Stuttgart. Although the senior member of the founder circle, he was one of the youngest in spirit.

Next to him in age came a Lutheran minister, August Pauli, who had supported more than one revolutionary move in the Lutheran church. In his quest he had resigned the ministry before the First War and later re-entered it. His was one of the clearest brains among us. Then there was Dr Rittelmeyer's younger brother Heinrich, the 'little' Rittelmeyer, as he was irreverently called. He had been principal of a teachers' training college and had made a big sacrifice in joining us.

One of the most colourful personalities was Professor Hermann Beckh. As a boy, in his school-leaving examination, he had done so brilliantly that in his year he was one of the best four in the kingdom — Beckh was a Bavarian — who were customarily offered a place at the Maximilianeum in Munich. This was a residential hall of the University, one of Munich's monumental buildings, in which those who qualified were for four years the guests of the King, with all expenses paid. It was popularly known as *die Ministerschule,* because it was normally regarded as a safe first stepping stone to an eventual seat in the Bavarian cabinet, or at least to a Permanent Under-Secretaryship. Beckh read law, and while still in his early thirties

Hermann Beckh (1875-1937), lawyer and professor of oriental languages.

Wolfgang Schickler (1894-1960), soldier and later portrait painter.

he was appointed to a junior judgeship. Then suddenly he threw everything overboard and started once more from the beginning, this time studying oriental languages. He was soon at the top again, and became professor of oriental languages at the University of Berlin. He specialized in Tibetan and was a member of the team which published the first Tibetan dictionary. In connection with this work he spent some time in London. When he resigned from the University to join us, the authorities were scandalized, and made every effort to hush it up. As is customary for a professor, Beckh wrote many books, before and after he entered our circle. His comprehensive study of Buddhism still runs into new editions. Beckh was also an accomplished musician, and wrote a fascinating work on the metaphysical qualities of the musical keys. He was a confirmed bachelor, and altogether what the Germans call *ein Original.* It was a sad blow to our movement when he died in 1937.

Another remarkable character was an ex-cavalry officer, Schickler. When the defeat of Germany ended his service in the army, he made a name for himself as a portrait painter. In his early years as a priest he supported himself and his big family by accepting now and then a commission for a portrait. Some leading figures of the Weimar Republic sat for him. There were

The original international leadership of The Christian Community, Emil Bock (who succeeded Rittelmeyer as head of the Community in 1938), Friedrich Rittelmeyer and Johannes Werner Klein.

also one or two people with a business background who had come into the anthroposophical movement as lecturers for the Threefold Social Order* and whose human and social interests drew them into the religious field.

Coming now to the younger group, the majority consisted of students — postgraduates and undergraduates — mainly from the Universities of Berlin and Marburg which contributed the scholar type, and from the University of Tübingen which provided more the community man and the missionary. The outstanding figure among the Berlin group was Dr (L. Th.) Emil Bock. He was a curate at the time. I remember him standing in the pulpit of his church in the usual black Lutheran cassock preaching an impatient and peremptory sermon during an evening service. It must have been one of his last, perhaps his very last, appearance as a Lutheran minister. Invalided out of the war, his academic studies had ranged, like those of other members of the founder circle, over a variety of fields including mathematics, languages and history. He brought into the foundation not only a mind of rare comprehensiveness, but also immense industry and courage. Besides, whilst nearly all the

* The Threefold Social Order was the name of an independent movement for social, political and economic reform which endeavoured to apply Rudolf Steiner's ideas to public affairs.

other founders came from middle class homes, Emil Bock added to the movement from the beginning the gravity and drive of a working class background. When Friedrich Rittelmeyer died in March 1938 Emil Bock succeeded him as head of The Christian Community. Under the Nazi terror he spent nine months in a concentration camp. I believe he secured an unusually early release through sheer force of personality. Outstanding is his monumental series of books interpreting the spiritual history of mankind as seen through the books of the Old and New Testament.

Marburg, a lovely small University town in the heart of Germany, clustered round the hill with the castle which was once the home of St. Elizabeth of Hungary, contributed another handful of young scholars. It included Dr Rudolf Frieling, who succeeded as head of the movement after Bock's death in December 1959.

The Tübingen set to which I belonged and about which I can speak from closer personal knowledge represented a different type. Nearly all of us had roots in the original, pre-war German Youth Movement. Many attempts have been made to describe this movement and its history but none has quite succeeded. It is difficult to convey the fact that in the first decade of the century a spontaneous movement among schoolboys and schoolgirls sprang up in many parts of Germany, at first uncoordinated but inspired by the same impulses and ideals, which revolutionized the life of many German teenagers in the teeth of a puzzled, disapproving and often hostile generation of parents and teachers. My own life as a schoolboy from about fifteen years onwards was completely absorbed in it; everything else took second place and appeared dated and second-rate. We continued to go to school in a more or less routine fashion and managed to pass our examinations; but for all that our 'real' life was centred elsewhere and school became rather irrelevant. We had a great sense of mission, and somehow groped for true values amidst a civilization which worshipped money, power and the ritual of drink, and of which the schools were an integral part.

In Rudolf Steiner we met a member of the older generation who understood what we were groping for. In his work we found thoughts which could explain us to ourselves and raise into consciousness our half-conscious promptings. In his teaching we discovered an objective sanction for the way of life we

Wilhelm Kelber (1901-67) came, like Heidenreich, through the Youth Movement which had led him into an active political life.

Friedrich Doldinger (1897-1973), like Beckh, an original character — poet, dramatist, painter, musician, besides a creative theological mind.

were after, at an important turning-point of history. We learned to see that ultimately our wanderlust was a material projection of the Quest for the Grail. In terms of numbers it was of course only a few who recognized Steiner at the time. But a first meeting with him of representatives of the Youth Movement, on Palm Sunday 1921, was a historic event. On the human level it was so gripping and electrifying that afterwards we danced in the street to the astonishment of the normal citizens on their afternoon walk. Under this impact I ventured on a small book *Jugendbewegung und Anthroposophie.* It was the sort of beginner's book about which one blushes ever after, but at the time its 5,000 copies were sold quickly, and to this day I meet people who tell me that this little book was their first introduction to Rudolf Steiner.

An outstanding figure among those who came into the founder circle from the Youth Movement was a young man called Wilhelm Kelber. He emerged as a national figure during the turbulent months which followed the collapse of the Imperial Reich. In spite of his youth, he had a presence and a degree of personal authority which to my mind could only be understood in terms of a previous life. At the age of nineteen he was called into the Ministry of Education in Berlin as an official adviser on youth affairs. In those earliest days of its existence, the Weimar Republic made a brave effort to provide room for the ideals of the Youth Movement and to enlist its forces for the rebuilding of a new Germany. Alas, very soon factional interests took hold of this attempt. Nationalist, socialist, Communist, Catholic, Protestant and other sectional 'youth movements' were launched from above, political or denominational programmes were superimposed, and the energies of the younger generation pushed into the old channels. It was a tragic mistake, a historic miscarriage, and Wilhelm Kelber soon resigned from his post in the Ministry of Education.

This variety of personalities assured for the founder circle a powerful range and scope; also a certain historic rightness. Christianity has always contained polar opposites: conservatives and progressives, scholars and missionaries, mystics and pioneers, Dominicans and Franciscans. But in the founder circle of The Christian Community the polarity went even further; it included not only enthusiasts and scholars, but Christians and 'pagans'. Some of the older generation were indeed profoundly convinced Christians; but some of the younger generation had no use for Christianity as they met it in the churches or in other forms. I cannot remember myself ever having gone to church for religious reasons after my fifteenth year. I went once to a service in the army, but never again. I may have been an extreme case, but certainly no exception. If it had not been for Steiner, those like myself would never have found a way to Christ. He showed us the Christ as a cosmic spiritual being, through whose indwelling in the human soul man could find his self-consciousness and self-awareness in harmony with God. 'I in them and Thou in me, that they may be made perfect in one.' As a statement of cosmic relationships this Johannine sentence made sense. But it was only gradually that we accepted also the historic Jesus of the Gospels. It was again Steiner who opened our eyes.

Of course, such polarities among the founders also created tensions. It was no mean task to weld this circle into a unit. Rudolf Steiner helped us to sort out our differences like a true and wise father. Apart from his understanding heart and practical common sense, he had more profound sources at his disposal. He possessed first-hand insight into the facts of reincarnation and the laws which govern this metaphysical reality (which seems today to be assumed instinctively as a fact by a steadily growing number of people). Steiner treated this subject with the greatest discretion. If anyone dared to speculate on, or in some form or other dabble in these deep things, he would be met with acid sarcasm or stern rebuke. But Steiner would speak from time to time in general terms and made it understandable — what in fact everybody knows in his heart — that it takes more than one life to become a Christian, if by being a Christian we mean the full penetration of a human being by Christ, and not merely an acceptance of certain ideas and feelings of veneration for him.

In the very last months of his activity, in his most mature lectures, Rudolf Steiner went just a small step further than he had ever done before. He described the differences of past lives which work themselves out in men and women who are drawn into the new Christian revelation today. Some carry with them a 'Platonic', others an 'Aristotelian' background from a former life. For reasons arising from this past, some are drawn in the first place to the new spiritual cosmology which opens up today and they will eventually accept Christ as the coping stone of the universe; others are looking for a new and direct approach to Christ and accept the 'cosmic' aspect of the new dispensation only gradually. Some among the seekers of today have had already a 'Protestant' incarnation and strive now for a higher harmony of the Catholic and Protestant positions, others need first to pass through a Protestant phase before they will go further.

We gathered that these historic tensions were at work as undercurrents in the depths of our own souls. The realization of this explained some of the clashes of opinion with which we surprised and shocked one another. It did not make these clashes less vivid, but it took the sting out of them, and pointed the way to new and creative harmonies.

Among the new factors was the presence of women in full equality. Never before in the history of Christianity had there been women priests, fully ordained and authorized to administer all sacraments. By including women into the succession of the new priesthood, Rudolf Steiner had sanctioned a step of far-reaching consequence. He expressed the hope that they would bring their womanly quality into the new office, and not

Kelber, Lenz, Perthel, Husemann and Bock, just before the war, in which both Lenz and Perthel lost their lives.

simply adopt the traditional masculine pattern. We were not blind to the fact that the priesthood of women presented a stumbling block to certain sections of Christian theology, but we had no doubt that this theology should be rethought in the light of the new understanding of the facts of human development.

Two more among the founders must be mentioned by name. Their life and work carried the promise of a special future: Johannes Perthel and Eduard Lenz. Johannes Perthel had been a Protestant minister in Saxony before the First World War. His experience of some of the most depressing industrial conditions of Germany caused him, after the war, to throw in his lot with the German Labour Movement. He became an active worker in the German Social Democratic Party. At the foundation of The Christian Community his quiet maturity marked him out for a leading position, and he became a member of the original body of seven office-holders. First from Breslau in Silesia, and later from Leipzig in Saxony he exercised his duty of regional leadership and co-ordination in Eastern Germany. Eduard Lenz was equally linked with the eastern centres of our Community. The founding of The Christian Community in Czechoslovakia, together with Josef Kral, was his historic achievement. Eduard Lenz had only just completed his twenty-first year when the foundation took place. Mature beyond his years, he was already married and father of a son. In the Czech Journal of The Christian Community for which he wrote copiously from its start in 1927 to its suppression in 1941, he left a rich legacy from which to this day translations are made for the German and English journals.

Johannes Perthel was killed in an air raid in 1944. Eduard Lenz whose love went out to the eastern peoples of Europe, particularly to the true Russia, was taken prisoner by the Russians in Czechoslovakia, deported to the Siberian coal mines, and died from exhaustion on a transport near Omsk in November 1945.

In Perthel and Lenz our movement lost two leaders who, in their way, have been irreplaceable. But we have tried to read the hieroglyphics which Providence has written on the wall. Were not these two men the chosen leaders of our eastern centres where no real work is possible at this time? 'Russia, in her present state [1923], is a field of purgatory not a field for spiritual activities', Rudolf Steiner is reported to have said. But the Christian renewal behind the Iron Curtain is not cancelled for ever, it is only suspended. And our two departed friends may well be among the trustees of a future which is maturing now in the spiritual world, and which in the fullness of time will surely descend when altars for the new revelation of Christ will also be planted among the Slav peoples.

And now let us return once more to the lakeside at Breitbrunn, mentioned already in the previous chapter, where the founders first faced up to their extraordinary diversity and discovered their unity. Breitbrunn was quiet, beautiful and — cheap. The long chain of the Bavarian Alps looked down on us from the distance with clearcut features or in misty outlines, according to the weather; and the undulating hills of the neighbourhood with their fields and forests sheltered us as in a cradle. The village was very small, and the conditions very rural. The German mark had begun to rush downhill on its inflationary spin, and we were all very poor.

I cannot remember how other members of the circle maintained themselves. We didn't ask each other much about our economics. I cannot even recall exactly on what I was living at the time. A very modest allowance from my father had come to an end when he died on New Year's Day 1922. I had kept going by addressing envelopes at night, working as a farm labourer in the holidays, and an occasional afternoon as a film 'extra' during term time.

Our organizing hostess, Frau Margarete Morgenstern, had spared no effort to explore every possible kind of accommodation that the little place could offer. The younger members made do in barns, on hay or straw, with the threshing floors as dressing rooms. I was given preferential treatment as I was still working on my doctor's thesis at the time: a bed in the loft of a bakery, directly over the large oven. The rural charm was represented by an army of cockroaches which, attracted by the warmth of the oven, assembled nightly on the wooden planks and the sloping rafters over my head. I never knew whether they would pay a visit to my bed during the night. It took some effort to wrench my mind away from these weird and unprepossessing creatures before going to sleep.

Our meeting place was an empty byre, with a vaulted ceiling and real windows. The built-in feeding troughs were filled with straw and served as seats, supplemented by a collection of chairs kindly lent by the local peasants. In the centre a table was improvised with a few rough boards. Decorated with green branches and a few prints, the byre made a cool and friendly assembly hall quite suitable for a gathering of new poverellos.

(The building still exists, although it has been divided into two sections. The owners are quite used to showing visitors round who come on a pilgrimage to 'the stable'. It can easily be reached from Munich and is not far from Oberammergau with its Passion Play. In fact, Ober*ammer*gau takes its name from the river which feeds the *Ammer*see.)

There we met day after day for two weeks, read the text of the Act of Consecration of Man which we had no authority yet to celebrate, treated each other to little addresses and discussions, and nursed our plans and wishful thoughts for the future. The difference of our age levels was strikingly obvious; it seemed also to go through each one of us individually. Rudolf von Koschützki has described what he felt when he first appeared in

The simple interior of the stable at Breitbrunn where the founding group met before going for the foundation events in Dornach.

our circle. 'I found myself in a curious dilemma. When I looked at a speaker, I said to myself: this is a student; but when I closed my eyes I had to say to myself: this is a professor, not an imitation but a real one, who speaks with expert knowledge and modesty. I have never met such a curious assembly in my life.' From the vantage point of his fifty-six years Koschützki could observe what we younger ones certainly were not conscious of. But for the record let it be said that during the rest of the day we were anything but professors. Fiddle, flute and guitar took over in the evening, and the lake echoed with our songs.

One day Michael Bauer came to visit us in a small horse-drawn carriage. It was said that he had only a small part of his lungs left, not greater than the palm of a hand. His visit was a token of his love for us and our aims; 'a last flickering of an altar-candle, which had been consumed in the sacred act of living' — as someone put it.

For the last Sunday morning an open-air service was planned to which some friends from Munich and the neighbourhood were invited. In general we treated our gathering as off the record and ourselves as incommunicado. But towards the end some friends and well-wishers were to be drawn in. I asked a friend who was a master on the guitar and who played Bach preludes for our service. We sat in a clearing of the woods, and now Dr

Rittelmeyer spoke. I remember only one sentence: 'Lake and mountains greet us and wish us well.' I had been asked to follow Rittelmeyer as one of the younger ones. I had never done such a thing, but hammered out in my mind a kind of fairy tale about bread and wine. And I simply told that story. It fell on most receptive ears. I had to write it down, and it is still being reprinted in various papers.

Apart from the building another visible memento of these weeks of preparation is a photograph of the circle of founders, taken in the little open space in front of the byre. During the last war I showed it to a Canadian friend who worked as staff sergeant in the photographic section of the Canadian H.Q. in London. He asked for a loan of my copy and one day surprised us with a series of impressive enlargements and a number of smaller reproductions which have since given much joy and amusement to many. The original amateur photographer did not find it too easy to get so many faces into a small picture, and the result is not a photographic masterpiece. But there we are, held fast as we were in August 1922, for history to look at.

On September 5 we rose at dawn. The older gentlemen had crossed the lake by the last steamer the night before. It was not only a romantic urge which prompted us to row ourselves across at sunrise in boats which some local friends would take back. We must have been seven or eight boats, and I can still see with the eye of memory the slow-moving convoy, drawn out across the lake. I am sure that none of us thought at the time of the fishermen of Galilee. But was it really blasphemous if, in later years, the comparison sometimes flashed through our minds? And when forty-one years later I sat on the shore of the Lake of Galilee near the place where scholars think that the village of Bethsaida must have been, was it surprising that the image of the Ammersee rose up in my mind, as I looked across to the other side and the mountains of the Golan?

The Ammersee had been the first lake I had ever seen in my life. We passed it in the train when I was eight years old, and my parents took me for the first time on a journey. Later, in my student days, I spent happy hours in the house of friends at the lake shore; and one Sunday in February, returning from a ski-tour, we had plunged into its icy water. Now another dimension took over. Unseen forces of incomprehensible magnitude began to take hold of us and to put us into our places.

Mythology entered our lives, and for a while we could see ourselves and each other only as in a waking dream.

The journey to Dornach was, however, realistic enough. We could only afford the cheapest trains. Today one can fly from Munich to Basle in twenty-five minutes. Our journey took twelve hours. The railway line crosses repeatedly from Germany into Switzerland, and back and forth again. It was built in the happy days of peace and goodwill, when frontiers mattered little. But in 1922 we had to leave the train with our luggage at every frontier station. Like a herd of cattle we were driven through passport controls and Customs examinations until at long last we arrived at Basle, and with a final effort dragged our luggage across the town to the tram which should take us to Dornach.

3 Faith and Order

In the article in *Das Goetheanum* of 1923, quoted in chapter 1, Rudolf Steiner referred to the founders as 'German theological students'. This was a somewhat sweeping generalization. Ten of the older group were no longer 'students' and twenty of the younger ones were students of other subjects. Few of them could have fancied themselves as ordinary theological students, unless in a nightmare.

The truth of the matter was, of course, that 'theological students' was the appropriate general description for the position which we assumed in relation to Rudolf Steiner. Before him we were all 'theological students'. Theology, though understood in a vastly more comprehensive sense than usual, was the subject matter which he treated before us. A great deal of new theology was needed if we were to attempt a Christian renewal.

Later, in his last published reference to The Christian Community,* Rudolf Steiner called us 'candidates for an honest and spiritually real priesthood'. This was more forward-looking. For this, it did not matter what job we had had in the past, what studies we had pursued, what academic labels we had acquired. Candidates for a new Christian priesthood — this was the category into which we were to grow in the future. It was our assignment with history.

The shift of emphasis from theology to priesthood was of the essence of the situation. Many a time had a 'new theology' arisen and been taught in the history of Christianity. A new priesthood never. But we were destined to be just this; not lecturers or

* *Mitteilungsblatt*, October 5, 1924.

teachers of a new theology, but a new order of priests who were to celebrate the Christian sacraments reborn from their original source. And now we must attempt an outline of this new faith and order, and we shall not be able to avoid altogether getting into deeper waters.

Ritual, according to Steiner, is a legitimate means of communicating with the unseen half of our world, of active relationship with the divine spiritual background of our existence, the kingdom of God. There may be many ways for the individual soul of making contact with the world of spirit through prayer and meditation. But communally there is nothing which in its reality is on the same level with ritual.

It is a fact that the appearance of Christ sharply divides pre-Christian and Christian ritual. In pre-Christian times ritual, which was very varied in form but universal in fact, demonstrated the deeper truths of life in liturgical pictures for the masses of the faithful. In Greece the 'sacred drama of Eleusis' presented the tragic loss by Demeter of her daughter Persephone to Hades, or Pluto, the god of the underworld. The parable of Isis, the goddess widowed through the murder of her husband Osiris, and the rescue of Isis by her son Horus, was a universal focussing point of religious thought and feeling in Egypt. In the Near East the cult of Adonis put before the devotees a picture of death and resurrection. In each one of these and many other similar rites the vital truth was taught in picture form, that the world of man has fallen into the grip of the dark powers of evil and destruction, but that this fallen world can be rescued and one day rise again. Perhaps it is beyond our powers of imagination, and certainly beyond our normal experience, to form an adequate picture of the shattering impact which these pictorial ceremonies must have had on those who witnessed them.

However, these ceremonies were only symbolic representations, outward and visible signs. They were the esoteric translations of the first-hand inspiration and secret knowledge possessed by the initiates. The esoteric events themselves, that is the direct intercourse with the spiritual world in full reality was strictly confined to the inner circle of the priests and initiates. They alone performed, in the inner sanctuary, the occult sacrifices through which the god appeared.

In contrast, Christian — 'post-Christ' — ritual is not merely a pictorial demonstration of metaphysical truths, although this plays into it. It is demonstration and real act all at once. The Christian Sacrament is the actual communication with the spirit-world in reality but this act of communication is not reserved for a secret society of officiating priests. It is open to all practising Christians. Christianity is a mystery religion in the sense that it communicates with the unseen but not in the sense that this is the privilege of a secret brotherhood of initiates.

In the fullness of time Christ stepped out of the unseen half of the world into the visible, and forged the essential link between the two. It is in his name that Christians continue to maintain this link in their sacraments. This is the significance of 'the New Covenant'. Its origin lies in the dual being of Christ, his divine and human nature. At the Last Supper his historic human presence 'instituted' the breaking of the bread and the sharing of the wine; after his resurrection he 'inspired' the further use and development of this rite. In the Last Supper, before his death, Christ observed the ritual of his own people. 'It becomes us to fulfil all righteousness'. The Passover, too, was more than an act of remembrance. The exodus from Egypt which it commemorated had been, for all its historic fact, a sacred drama with a deeper meaning: 'Out of Egypt have I called my son'. After his resurrection Christ adopted and sanctioned also other rites. Rudolf Steiner made the astonishing statement that during the forty days between Resurrection and Ascension Christ walked spiritually through the mystery temples of the ancient world. Thus the sacrament of the Eucharist has ultimately grown from two sources: the Last Supper and the mystery temples. The process of this growth defies detailed analytical research, unless it can be observed by a higher consciousness.

Such, put here in very condensed terms, was the spiritual *history* of sacramental ritual, as we learned it from Rudolf Steiner. But there was also a sacred *science* of ritual to be learned. It concerned the redemption of man from his fallen state.

Man commits individual sins. Time and again he falls from grace. He pulls himself up and he falls again. Goethe was no exceptional monster when he confessed: 'there is no crime of which I would not have been potentially capable'. And which honest person has not said many times in his life, 'There, but for the grace of God . . .'?

However, all this is only one half of the case, the individual, personal, *subjective* side of sin. But there is also an *objective* side to it, which the average man or woman hardly ever considers because it is obscured by current scientific teaching and the popular views of evolution. Natural man, even if he leads a moral life and is in good health, is nevertheless *objectively* shot through with 'sin'. Natural functions which we take for granted and normal, reveal to the deeper insight that they have been affected by a 'fall'.

Close the doors and windows tightly in a room in which a company of men and women are assembled, and they will asphyxiate each other in a short time simply by breathing. We breathe in the breath of life and breathe out the breath of death. Eastern religions have been acutely aware of this disturbing reality. In the West such facts have long been dismissed from religious considerations, ever since St. Augustine formulated a doctrine which excluded nature and natural things from the scheme of salvation. Consider man's sexual life. The real cause of the embarrassment which we feel when sexual matters are discussed in public is the fact that through a 'fall' man's sexual life has come nearer to that of the animal kingdom than was intended by the Creator. A study of our digestive functions leads to a similar conclusion. Compare our blood with the 'innocent' sap of the rose and you will sense that it is charged with egotism; it is hot and passionate. Even our sense organs — eyes, ears, nose — betray to a more subtle science of physiology that they destroy the fullness of impressions before they can register them.

The sum total of these facts is contained in a traditional term, now usually completely incomprehensible even to practising Christians, namely 'original sin'. It refers to an 'original', universal family sickness in the human race, of which the above-mentioned symptoms are evidence, and in which we all partake, willy-nilly, simply by being born into it. In this sense it is factually true that we are 'born in sin'. Not the act of birth is sinful, nor the sexual act which causes birth. But it is the earthly human nature into which we are born in the normal process of incarnation which is basically sick, which partakes of the 'sickness of sin'. The final result of this sickness is physical death. 'The wages of sin is death.' But not death as such, (that is the change of one form of existence into another) but the fact that we leave a decomposing carcass behind instead of being able to dissolve it into creative energy — as, for the first time, Christ did at Easter — when our time on earth has run its course.

Christ's universal redemptive act is concerned with the whole range of these conditions of fallen humanity. Salvation in Christ is an evolutionary process which ultimately embraces the body as well as the soul. Step by step, at the imperceptible pace of Providence, Christ's redemptive activity is at work in those who turn to him. This, not Christ's teaching, is the unique and distinctive quality of the Christian religion.

In this the sacrament is an integral part. It is the medicine which we can take against original sin. It offers us the chance of being integrated into the stream of grace. It links the practice of religion with the cosmic process, and so gives objective significance to the act of worship. It makes religion real beyond the subjective experience.

With great patience Rudolf Steiner unfolded these matters before us. He must have known that we understood only a fraction. But he trusted that the seed would grow. It would grow and mature under the golden rays of the very sacrament of the altar with which Providence had entrusted him, that he might bring it down to us; the sacrament of communion reborn, refreshed, rejuvenated from its eternal archetypal pattern, descending into the thirsting wilderness of our age.

Life with the sacrament in its renewed form, and experience of its power, would also shed new light on the Bible. It is common knowledge that during the nineteenth century the Bible became the object more of criticism than of reverence, certainly among many theologians. In my schooldays the so-called 'higher criticism' had arrived in the classroom. Christ had become 'the simple man of Nazareth'. It was the picture at which the blind intellectual honesty of the scholars had finally arrived. It took the core out of Christianity and left only the husks. We boys could not be enthusiastic about a pious carpenter who may have said things a little better than other founders of religions before him, and who may have died for his convictions as other people had done before and after him. 'Why should we worship a dead Jew?' was the poignant question of a bewildered generation, misled by its pastors, before it became the blasphemous battle cry of the Nazis. Matters have never been carried to such lengths in England as they were driven by the too thorough Germans, but basically the tendency was the same. It was in fact universal.

It is true that in recent years the tide has begun to turn — among theologians. It is reported that in particular some of the German Lutheran ministers in their epic struggle of resistance against the Nazi tyranny rediscovered the Bible and found in it 'what God has to say to man'. The whole marvellous spate of new translations into modern languages and the modern idiom, also reflects the new interest. But will a mere new habit of Bible reading alone be enough, even if it ever came to that? While writing this I saw a report of a public address by an eminent Member of Parliament in which he said: 'I know of no book which has been a source of brutality and sadistic conduct, both public and private, that can compare with the Bible.' I am afraid this is a perfectly defensible conclusion, if the Bible is taken simply as a handbook of Christian conduct. History would bear out what he has said. And it would be a dangerous fallacy if we believed that new translations alone would make much difference.

We need new light on the Bible; a light which can never come from the Bible itself alone. There is indeed an inexhaustible wealth of new working material in Steiner's books and lectures. But life with the sacrament is a *constant and ever present* fresh source of light particularly for the New Tastament. The sacrament speaks from the same source from which the Gospels have been inspired. It trains the ear for the overtones and undertones of Holy Scripture.

Strange as it may appear, it is the experience of the cosmic Christ in the sacrament which leads to a new grasp of the historic Jesus in the Gospels. Christ explains Jesus, for this is the true order of experience. We begin to understand the inexpressibly great sacrifice which Christ made in becoming Jesus. We sense the suffering of his being made man. And we feel powerless to gauge the immensity of his Passion.

This Christ we can love. It is pathetic to ask that anyone should love the carpenter of Nazareth. But the Christ Jesus we can love with all our hearts. 'If we learn to love the Christ Jesus with the same intensity as we love our parents, husband or wife, or our children, we shall know what selfless love is.' This also is a saying of Steiner, and it disposes of the mistaken view that he was a 'neo-gnostic' who understood only the cosmic Christ.

In an inspired sentence the late John Middleton Murry expressed his belief of what the new age of Christianity would be

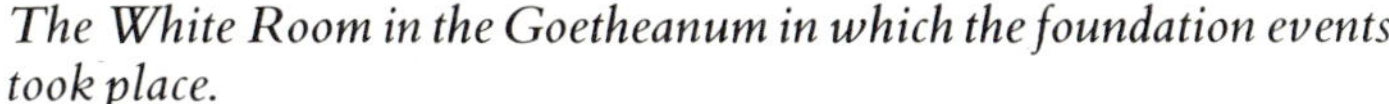

The White Room in the Goetheanum in which the foundation events took place.

The carved rostrum used as the first altar.

like. 'The holding together,' he wrote, 'in a single act of understanding, of the historic Jesus and the cosmic Christ, is probably the distinctive act of the re-edified Christian Church. But it can hardly be expected of more than a tiny minority.' If Middleton Murry had been with us at Dornach, he could have observed that his prophecy was beginning to be fulfilled before he uttered it.

During three to four hours a day we were closeted with Steiner and occupied with these weighty matters. We met in the so-called White Room, an upper room in the south wing of the first Goetheanum where the builders were still busy. We had to climb an improvised temporary staircase and cross unfinished floors to get to our room, which was panelled all round and, as mentioned before, lit only by a skylight. One whole wall consisted of built-in cupboards in which some eurythmists of the Goetheanum kept their dresses. At the back a narrow staircase led to a minstrels' gallery on which Frau Marie Steiner at times sat and shared in our meetings.

In a sense we led a double life. For during the remaining hours of the day we gave ourselves up to the usual life at Dornach. Dornach can be indescribably beautiful in September. The peak of the summer heat which can be stifling is past, the gardens are bursting with flowers, a cool breeze comes from the mountains, and every tree and object stands out as clearly as possible. In that September of 1922 Rudolf Steiner had arranged that people like

The first Goetheanum, designed by Rudolf Steiner, destroyed by fire three months after the foundation of The Christian Community.

us with a sick currency — *valutakrank* — should be supported by people with a healthy currency. Thus most of us were the guests of generous French anthroposophists. After the rigorous German austerities of the war and post-war years we revelled in real milk, real butter, white bread, cheese, real coffee and other long lost and almost forgotten delights. We made many friends who were profoundly interested in what was going on with us behind closed doors in the Goetheanum. But I am not quite sure that our unconcerned manners were always approved of by some ladies and gentlemen of grave mien and deportment, who we assumed were chiefly engaged in Developing Themselves.

4 The Christian Initiate of the West

What I have described so far is either the story of a collective fit of madness and even blasphemy, or of one of the greatest events in the history of Christianity. There is really no other alternative. As so much centres around the personality of Rudolf Steiner, still more must be said about him.

Had Rudolf Steiner lived in the Middle Ages, he would have been one of the great fathers of the Church. The Church was the universal font and home of all learning and knowledge, spiritual and secular. No spiritual genius, possessed even of the most far-reaching and comprehensive mental and spiritual powers, could have worked outside the Church. For Church and civilization were identical. At the beginning of the twentieth century the position was all but reversed. The Church, divided into innumerable separate units, big and small, was rapidly losing its influence. With the disappearance of most of the reigning princes on the continent of Europe, the last imposing façades also of ecclesiastical 'establishment' crumbled away, and religion departed as a serious influence from the life of those men and women who kept abreast of the times. Civilization had become secular. Although some Church functions remained in a decorative and social capacity, the scientific outlook penetrated into every nook and cranny of men's minds and became the accepted way of life.

It was natural that in this age the setting of Rudolf Steiner's work and his method of expression should be scientific. We

Rudolf Steiner (1861–1925).

should take too narrow a view, however, if we thought that he was simply conditioned by his environment and by the mental climate of his age. Men of Rudolf Steiner's spiritual rank, for whom adequate standards of comparison are difficult to find, are archetypal representatives, not products of their times. The sacred Genius of mankind himself ordains, as it were, that a great one should come when the time is fulfilled, and that he should unite himself in the fullest measure with the consciousness of his age in order to transform this consciousness from within, into its next stage of development.

When at the turning-point of the century Rudolf Steiner wrote into an almanac as his motto *In the place of God the free human being*, he voiced the deepest impulse of the time. With him this motto did not mean the 'abolition of God', as it might have meant with a lesser man. With him it meant the shedding of the last traces of dogmatic teaching, of deductive thought, the winding up of the last remnants of the legacy of the past, of the last forms of Scholasticism or Theosophy, whether Buddhist or Christian. In their place was to be developed an *inductive* approach to the spiritual world, proceeding step by step from the known to the unknown, an 'Anthroposophy' which discovering first the secrets of man would search eventually the deep secrets of God. Rudolf Steiner freely and consciously walked the way down the ladder of consciousness into the dark abyss of pure brain-bound intellect, and across the threshold to the rebirth of cosmic intelligence in man himself. Through this, man could rediscover himself in freedom as a spiritual being and a companion of the heavenly hierarchies.

This could be achieved if the recognized scientific training of the day were turned into a spiritual exercise. In an almost extreme degree Rudolf Steiner describes this austere method in the last chapter of *The Riddles of Philosophy.*

> The ideas . . . of the modern scientific method, present the best subject matter for mental exercises in which the soul can immerse itself, and on which it can concentrate in order to free itself from its bondage to the body. Whoever uses these natural scientific ideas in the manner that has been outlined above, will find that the thoughts that first seem to be meant to depict only natural processes will really set the soul free from the body. Therefore, the spiritual science that is here referred to must be seen as a contamination of the scientific way of thinking provided it is inwardly experienced in the right way.*

By developing this path with unheard-of energy and consistency throughout his life, Rudolf Steiner became a true 'Scientist of the Invisible'.† In other words, he became the first initiate of the west, the first independent occult teacher in the Christian era. Rudolf Steiner turned the sphere of revelation into a sphere of discovery. In the fifteenth century some people *believed* that the earth was a globe, and that land was beyond the Atlantic. But Columbus *went* there. Up till now, many people *believed* that there was a world of the spirit. But Steiner *went* there.

It was a matter of course that his research and his discoveries in the supersensible should extend to matters which are of the profoundest interest to religion, that is to the *personal relationship* of the human soul and spirit to the higher powers and beings. But Rudolf Steiner did not consider it as part of his own mission to enter himself into the field of organized religion. In a public lecture at Liestal in Switzerland, given on January 11, 1916 (incidentally one of the best introductions to new enquirers) he

Correction p.61, 1.21 should read:

. . . must be seen as a continuation of the . . .

* *The Riddles of Philosophy*, Anthroposophic Press Inc, Spring Valley, NY, 1973, p.456.

† The title of an account of Steiner's personality and work by Canon A. P. Shepherd, D.D. (Hodder & Stoughton, 1954).

defined his attitude by saying, 'Spiritual Science can, of course, go so far as to consider the spiritual phenomena which have appeared as religion in the course of the world's evolution. But Spiritual Science can never desire to create a religion any more than natural science indulges in the illusion of being able to create something in nature.'

Rudolf Steiner observed this principle quite strictly. He never indulged 'in the illusion' of desiring 'to create a religion'. But to refrain from 'creating a religion' was one thing; to help in arresting the decline of Christian life and worship another. As he once said to Dr Rittelmeyer, 'The fact that I possess clairvoyant faculties is nothing so very special; but that I know what Christianity needs today — this indeed is grace.'*

Towards the end of the First World War, Steiner began to describe in more precise terms what he held to be necessary for the future of Christian life and worship. One lecture, which he gave at Dornach on October 13, 1918 as part of a series on the history of mankind, may serve as an example. He speaks in this context of the ritual of the Mass, 'a picture of the highest mysteries of all time', which has grown old in the Catholic tradition, tied to an outworn form of consciousness, and which must be renewed. 'One should feel,' he says, 'how amidst the events which have led to this terrible world-catastrophe, the need for ritual has grown again among human beings . . . What has been preserved from ancient times but in part has been thoroughly worn out in the course of human life, presents itself as a fresh need: the need of human beings for sacramental acts, for spiritual forms. To behold in these forms the divine life in the world, but also to *understand* these forms, this is what we need.' In these and similar statements some of the central features of the future Christian Community were anticipated by him. When, therefore, through the enquiry of the founders of the Community the historic opportunity arose for him to play a decisive part in the renewal of the practice, and indeed the very heart of Christianity, with people who felt a call and were prepared to carry responsibility themselves, he was instantly ready to act with the full wealth of his initiate knowledge and with the full authority of his spiritual stature.

It is difficult to say when it first occurred to Rudolf Steiner that a call of this kind might be coming to him. He moved according to judgments and directions above the level of that of ordinary

* Quoted in *Die Christengemeinschaft*, II, p.22.

men. But from the way in which he spoke in later years it appears that he must have seen the potential form and being of The Christian Community descend from the spiritual world increasingly clearly before it eventually took physical shape on earth. Particularly in the last months of his life — as if he was conscious of his approaching death — he undertook to lift part of the curtain which normally covers and hides the superhuman powers and super-earthly events of history. As already mentioned in chapter 2, he began to disclose the spiritual-historic background of the anthroposophical movement and of the souls of its first bearers. They are souls, he said, who before they descended into earthly incarnation had gathered in the spiritual world around the Archangel Michael, the standard-bearer of Christ, who prepared them for a far-reaching and crucial task. They were to serve on earth in the great historic break-through from the moon-like, reflective, intellectual thoughts which had increasingly ruled human civilization since the end of the Middle Ages, to the sun-like creative intuitive consciousness which can embrace on earth the realities of the invisible, and in particular the world of Christ. Among these souls, a vast cosmic ritual was celebrated at the turning point of the eighteenth to nineteenth century under Michael's guidance in the spiritual world. 'Super-sensible ritual acts, mighty pictures of spiritual life, of the cosmic beings, of the celestial hierarchies, linked with the great etheric activities of the cosmos and the human activities on earth' — this is how Rudolf Steiner described Michael's celebrations.* These sacred events form a background, indeed, for the whole of the anthroposophical movement; but they form also the cosmic womb out of which the sacramental rituals of The Christian Community were born.

It was consistent with the historic realities that from the beginning The Christian Community should stand on its own feet and that its leadership should be undertaken by a body of office-holders chosen from the circle of founders with Rudolf Steiner's close personal guidance, but independent of him in the exercise of their responsibilities. Rudolf Steiner himself did not assume any official position in The Christian Community. What he did and gave for The Christian Community, he did and gave as 'private individual', and since this was not always adequately understood, he said so at times with emphasis.

As a 'private individual' he conducted himself also in his

* Lecture of September 16, 1924.

relationship to the functions of The Christian Community once it was founded. He treated it without compromise as the nucleus of the Christian Church in the Age of the renewed 'etheric' presence of Christ. Before the foundation of The Christian Community he was willing, on occasion, to attend christenings, burials and other religious ceremonies carried out for members of the Anthroposophical Society by ministers of various denominations. After the foundation of The Christian Community he announced that in the future he would not do so unless the ceremony was carried out by a priest of The Christian Community, and he adhered to this rule without exception to the end of his life.

It was my privilege, as a young man, to conduct a marriage service in which Rudolf Steiner officiated as one of the two witnesses whom the ritual, as given through him, requires. Although I was sure of his full inward support as he followed everything with kind and solemn eyes, it was an unusual experience to speak to him the solemn words of admonition which the ritual addresses to the witnesses, and which say that they must never forget what they have seen and heard in this moment. I believe I spoke the words without hesitation, but with a sharp intake of additional mental breath! At the conclusion of the service Rudolf Steiner kissed the bride on her forehead and the bridegroom on both cheeks. It was a rare experience to see him move in circumstances where joy and solemnity mingled so naturally, where his greatness and his dignified humility were so evidently blended.

In 1924 Miss Edith Maryon, his close artistic collaborator, died. Rudolf Steiner telegraphed in person to the nearest priest of The Christian Community. It was a representative occasion, since Miss Maryon, the daughter of an English clergyman, was a member of the original *Vorstand* of the Goetheanum — the only English member of that body — and the head of the Section for the Formative Arts. Rudolf Steiner instructed the officiating priest with these words, 'You celebrate the ritual for the departed as a member of mankind. The ritual must come first. Then I follow and speak of the special conditions of life, which in this case were anthroposophical.'

It was natural that Rudolf Steiner's own burial should be conducted by The Christian Community at the request of Frau Marie Steiner, an event which Friedrich Rittelmeyer describes in a short, moving paragraph at the end of his book *Rudolf Steiner Enters my Life.*

The significance of Rudolf Steiner for Christianity is not confined to the foundation of The Christian Community. He was himself, simply as a being, an *event* in the history of Christianity. In the memorial article which Dr Rittelmeyer wrote after Rudolf Steiner's passing, he says:

> In earlier ages the fact alone that such an all-embracing genius gave witness to Christ as to the greatest reality in earthly history, would have had a profound effect. But in Rudolf Steiner much more was present. One could put it like this: he comprehended all branches of learning so spiritually and so deeply, and he recognized Christ in such big and broad dimensions that eventually Christ shines forth as the true light in all spheres of life. He observed strictly the necessity for each sphere to form its own method according to its intrinsic laws. He never carried religion into anything from without. But he illuminated all realms of knowledge with such powerful light, that Christ became visible in it. A Christ, it is true, far greater than the Christ of the Churches; but a Christ related to the Bible and to the Christ of the early Christians.
>
> Thus he advanced the science of language to the point where it could understand why Christ is called 'the Word'. Thus he carried medicine to the point where medicine could understand again 'the body of Christ'. Thus he carried astronomy to the point where Christ became visible as the true 'Light'. . . . he taught how science could again become reverent and devout. He built a temple for all sciences, so high and so broad, that their servants could work in it without sacrificing an iota of their personal freedom or of the special characteristics of their province. He united the learning of the age with Christ, and Christ with the learning of the age.*

Rittelmeyer's description opens up a vista for the future. The condition of the Middle Ages when Church and civilization were identical is not likely to be repeated. If it were, it would be a relapse into a past phase of evolution. We must move towards a future where *Christianity* and civilization become identical;

* *Die Christengemeinschaft,* Vol. II, p. 35.

where the very methods of scientific research will be Christian, and where it will be felt that what is not Christian is not scientific.

In this civilization the 'Church' will have its special place. Like the mother whose children have grown up and become independent, the Christian Church of the future will be able to concentrate on its particular task. It will practise *the personal meeting with Christ as a Being.* This will be all the more vital when Rudolf Steiner's teaching will be increasingly understood in which he explains why since Golgotha Christ must be found during man's life on earth. In its threefold office — prophetic, priestly and pastoral — the renewed Church will be the place where individual and community can *meet* the Christ. It will proclaim the Gospel with full spiritual understanding as Christ's abiding Word to mankind. It will administer the renewed sacraments as Christ's divine touch upon mankind, and will teach the practice of contemplation and prayer. It will heal the tragedies in men's lives and show forth Christ's forgiving and creative love.

This renewal The Christian Community has accepted as its historic task. For when it had, in fact, been shown that the new wine must be poured into new bottles, the initiate of the west entrusted The Christian Community with the new wine.

5 First Steps into the World

From headquarters the scene now shifts to the front. From Dornach, where we had been engrossed in the process of becoming priests, we went to our first action stations. From an upper room where we had sat together in community and had received the gifts of heaven, we dispersed and embarked on our first missionary efforts in the world.

The contrast was fierce. Dornach was an island of peace, almost like a colony of spirits outside time and space. Now we were to return like the knights of the Grail — very junior knights indeed — to the world which was considerably out of joint. Even on the purely material level the crossing of the frontier from Switzerland back into Germany was like moving from a prosperous residential suburb into a slum. A small personal experience may illustrate this. While in Dornach I had been put up by kind friends who lived a long way from the Goetheanum. One morning I was late; so my hosts gave me half a Swiss franc to pay for the tram fare. From a German point of view half a franc was a small fortune in those days. I confess that I accepted the gift, but saved it. I made the meeting in time by running a couple of miles. Afterwards that half franc, changed into German inflation marks, paid more than the fare for the express train all the way from Basle to Stuttgart.

Rudolf Steiner had been realistic enough to warn us of the uphill struggle which he saw ahead of us. He was particularly concerned about our livelihood. As we had decided to concentrate all our energies from the start on the foundation of free communities, and not to have any other job, it was not so easy to see what we were to live on. Steiner himself from the very first had spoken of the foundation of 'free communities' as 'the most beautiful way' of working for a Christian renewal. But he had also cautioned us in no uncertain terms concerning the heavy economic strain which it would entail. Happily, most of us were still young and unmarried, so that this prospect held no real terror. And we had long made up our mind to turn our back on whatever safe jobs our academic qualifications might open up for us, although usually the first and sometimes the only question asked by our professors, when we said good-bye, was: 'Who is going to pay you?'

However, I wonder how many people can really imagine what it means for a young man to start literally from scratch in a work of this kind. A simple account of my own first steps may illustrate the situation. I have warned readers before that this story is written from a personal angle, where excursions into autobiography cannot be altogether avoided. They supply graphic detail.

It had somehow emerged as agreed that I should begin and found a Christian Community at Frankfurt-on-Main. I had only been in Frankfurt once before in my life, on my return journey from prisoner-of-war camp, when I had wandered in its empty streets in the twilight of an early October morning in 1919, between the arrival of the train which had brought me to Frankfurt and the train which would take me home to Regensburg in Bavaria.

In the early twenties Frankfurt had close on half a million inhabitants. Although the town had been incorporated into Prussia in 1866, it had preserved a strong and independent tradition of its own, the roots of which went far into the past. I met families in whose memory Goethe, Frankfurt's most famous son, was still a live person, and among which his private life was still part of the family gossip — and strongly disapproved of. Among the leading citizens one would find great Huguenot names like Dubarry, Passavant, François. A French Calvinist Church was still going strong, with whose minister I soon became so friendly that together we conducted a study group in his church, and he offered us the hospitality of his church hall for our first midnight service at Christmas. On the outskirts of the town large industrial districts had been developed where the

German Dye Trust, the biggest single economic enterprise in Germany, built its enormous headquarters. But in the heart of the town the cathedral and the 'Roemer', the delightful medieval civic centre, were still intact (since pulverized by air-raids but reconstructed in the old style), where the young Goethe had witnessed the coronation of one of the last Emperors of the 'Holy Roman Empire of the German Nation'. Close by was the old Ghetto, where the original house of the Rothschilds still stood, from which 'the five Frankfurters' had gone out to found in the capitals of Europe the first international financial empire. Like all German towns of its size Frankfurt had its permanent Opera, with Clemens Kraus as the conductor at the time, and its permanent Symphony Orchestra which shared its conductor, Willem Mengelberg, with the Concertgebouw Orchestra of Amsterdam. Paul Hindemith added his revolutionary contemporary force to the musical life of the town. He himself played the viola in the quartet which usually gave the first performance of his chamber music works. The second violin player was a friend of the Community and played from time to time at our functions. To the art galleries a very lively colony of painters and sculptors was attached, among whom Fritz Beckmann was then the leading figure.

Of all this I knew nothing when I arrived with the first dark suit of my life as my only professional equipment. I had never before in my life given a public address except once to a gathering of youth, but I believed that the done thing was to start with public lectures. I had never read the Gospel of John, I had in fact the utmost difficulties in finding any relationship to it, yet I believed that I must take it as my subject. The first line of the prologue and the raising of Lazarus were the two chinks through which I could get a glimpse of the light enshrined in this unique document. So the first line of the prologue and the raising of Lazarus became my first two subjects, to which I added as a third one 'Bread and Wine'. In my enthusiasm I persuaded the printing manager of the *Frankfurter Zeitung*, to whom I had an introduction to print a supply of posters free of charge, and somehow I managed to have them displayed all over the town. Then I walked the streets for days and part of the nights with the one line in my head, 'In the beginning was the Word'. When the day of the first lecture came, the hall was respectably filled with about 150 people. I do not remember what I said, but I think the sheer

An early synod at Marienstein, Göttingen in summer 1924, including the host family (not named).

1. Hermann Beckh; 2. Marta Heimeran; 3. Johannes Hemleben; 4. Wilhelm Kelber; 5. Walter Gradenwitz; 6. Friedrich Doldinger; 7. Thomas Kändler; 8. Hermann Groh; 9. Fritz Blattmann; 10. Otto Franke; 11. Adolf Müller; 12. Carl Stegmann; 13. Robert Goebel; 14. Kaethe Wolf; 15. Karl Ludwig; 16. Jutta Frentzel; 17. Otto Becher; 18. Eberhard Kurras; 19. Rudolf Frieling; 20. Josef Kral; 21. Heinrich Rittelmeyer; 22. Karl Luttenberger; 23. Harald Schilling; 24. Rudolf Köhler; 25. August Pauli; 26. Heinrich Ogilvie; 27. Rudolf von Koschützki; 28. Ernst Moll; 29. Johannes Perthel; 30. Richard Gitzke; 31. Waldemaar Mickisch; 32. Martin Borchart; 33. Gertrud Spörri; 34. Ludwig Koehler; 35. Wilhelm Ruhtenberg; 36. Claus von der Decken; 37. Joachim Sydow; 38. Hermann von Skerst; 39. Hermann Fackler; 40. Arnold Goebel; 41. Rudolf Meyer; 42. Johannes Werner Klein; 43. Gottfried Husemann; 44. Gustav Spiegel; 45. Emil Bock; 46. Alfred Heidenreich; 47. Eduard Lenz; 48. Gerhard Klein; 49. Erwin Lang.

tension which lived in me must have communicated itself to the people, for the second lecture was overcrowded with about 350 people, the biggest audience that I managed to 'draw' for many years. Of course, I could not keep up the pace. At the third lecture the numbers dropped to eighty-five.

After the first evening I was happy to walk back to my lodgings with a cigar box full of bank notes, my first 'collection', with which I could pay my first debts. This had to be done immediately, for the German mark was then entering on its final crazy inflationary gallop, and a sum of money which one day would pay for a modest house might on the following morning be barely sufficient to buy a couple of rolls. It took me a long time to go to sleep that night. I lay awake with a palpitating heart and looked across the foot of my bed at a portrait of Johannes Valentinus Andreae which hung on the wall opposite, surrounded with pictures of his descendants, for quite accidentally and unknowingly I had rented a bed-sitter in the flat of some lineal descendants of that strange seventeenth century mystic who as a young man on the eve of the Thirty Years' War was inspired to write *The Chymical Wedding of Christian Rosenkreutz.*

My hostess was a remarkable lady of great character who had been the first woman member of the city council, on which once Goethe's father had sat. She died soon after my arrival, and rather surprisingly left word that I was to take her funeral. It was my first funeral service, and a great ordeal, since every conceivable public authority and society was represented at the service. After all, I was only twenty-five years old, and a complete newcomer and beginner.

However, to go back to my first venture as a lecturer, at the conclusion of the third meeting I stated what I had come to Frankfurt for, and also the economic truth, which was that I had come on faith. Would some people take turns in giving me one good meal a day; my needs were of the simplest and one good meal a day would keep me alive. The number of kind people who put their name on a list was big enough to arrange a fortnightly rota. Henceforth, and for all the six years I spent in Frankfurt, I took my main meal in the middle of the day with families of enquirers and later, members, who often invited friends, so that these invitations to lunch developed into veritable lunch-hour meetings. It was ruinous for the digestion, but marvellous for missionary work. Through a different method I tried to reach my contemporaries. With members of various youth groups I produced a medieval miracle play, with incidental music taken from Anton Bruckner's symphonies. It was a big undertaking, with a cast of thirty people. The local press published friendly reviews both of the lectures and of the play.

At long last, after about five months, the first Act of Consecration of Man could be celebrated. Seventeen people, carefully prepared, attended and became members there and then. For the first time in Frankfurt the body and blood of Christ was shared in the new dispensation. The local congregation of The Christian Community was thus founded on June 17, 1923 and henceforth the Act of Consecration of Man would be celebrated week after week. It had been difficult to find a room which I could afford; finally I decided on the Evangelical Workers' Union in a somewhat distant part of the town. It meant a walk of two and a half miles every Sunday there and back, with a heavy basket of equipment, too big to be allowed on a tram. A street sweeper, one of my first members, a really dear person, came every Sunday morning early and helped me. Between us we carried the basket on its two handles through the streets, and then spent a couple of hours in re-arranging the room and erecting the altar, for which in the end one or two ladies also helped. It was a somewhat exhausting preparation for the actual celebration, but it was all in a day's work.

More delicate than the outward problems was a peculiar inward problem which I had to solve. While from the very start I never felt any difficulty in celebrating the Act of Consecration, I had immense difficulties with the New Testament. In the celebration I felt myself from the beginning with great matter-of-factness as an alchemist who carried out certain sacred processess according to the instructions of the arch-alchemist, the Christ. This I could do with perfect conviction and dedication. But in spite of, or perhaps because of, a Lutheran upbringing I was positively allergic to the New Testament; it took me years to find an access to this, for me, alien territory. If this had been simply a personal oddity, I should pass it over in silence. But I think it was symptomatic. I may, again, have been an extreme case, but not an entire exception. I believe that some of us had to be complete newcomers to the traditional Christian documents, so as to make quite sure that they were rediscovered in complete freshness for the new age. The new springtide of Christianity could do with souls to whom nothing traditional seemed acceptable, if it was to be accepted simply for the sake of being traditional and time-honoured. If this movement was to do its divinely-ordained duty, there had to be something 'radically new' in it, to use a phrase which Rudolf Steiner repeatedly used with earnest emphasis.

For the time being, the one and only section from the New Testament which I could read with complete honesty was the fourth chapter of Revelation. And so for weeks my first patient fellow-worshippers had to listen to the same reading every Sunday. But really what more wonderful reading could we have had? Was it not the great apocalyptic vision of the throne, and the twenty-four elders, and the seven lamps burning before God, and the sea of glass, and the four archetypal beasts, and the heavens bursting forth into a paean of praise? Was it not a vision of our true and glorious home which earthly life and existence

A group of priests at Tübingen in 1950: Robert Goebel, Marta Heimeran, Ludwig Köhler, Gerhard Klein, Alfred Heidenreich.

had clouded, and which even in religion had become intellectual doctrine rather than vision, but which in our movement we were to unveil again and which we desired to proclaim with a new and sure voice?

While we thus made our first efforts as best we could, the public scene of German Central Europe underwent a significant change. War and defeat, and the aftermath of defeat, had shaken the people. Souls were ploughed up, and hungry for seed. The foundation of The Christian Community and our first efforts came just in time. Rudolf Steiner, in fact, warned us that we might be already a little too late. Soon the country settled down, and people sat back. At the end of 1923 the mark was stabilized, although with astronomical losses. With economic stabilization the old forces of nationalism, capitalism and militarism asserted themselves again, and absorbed and interests and active energies of many people. The extreme wings, Communist and National Socialist, began to marshal their ranks. Religious renewal was faced with a less sympathetic climate. But we had almost expected this and felt quite able to adapt ourselves to the new atmosphere, when difficulties arose from an unexpected quarter. The unexpected quarter was the Anthroposophical Society, and the difficulties caused by members of that body were by far the most serious ones and must be described in a separate chapter.

6 The Christian Community and the Anthroposophical Society

The Christian Community has, in a sense, a dual parentage. The historian of the future will regard it, I imagine, on the one hand as an offspring of the universal body of Christianity, as a coming together of those who first recognized Rudolf Steiner as a man sent from God and who through this recognition were led, with his help, to a new Christian dispensation. On the other hand, The Christian Community has grown out of the general anthroposophical movement. Steiner's lectures in Berlin, quoted in the first chapter, and subsequent meetings with Steiner, were its inciting cause. Nearly all the founders of The Christian Community were members of the Anthroposophical Society, and some of them held positions of responsibility. The Anthroposophical Society was the nursery in which our impulse had been reared. We felt ourselves as that branch of the anthroposophical movement which 'carried the knowledge of the spirit into religious experience' (compare p.33). It was, therefore, inevitable at the beginning that the life of the young Christian Community should have been vitally affected by the condition of the Anthroposophical Society and its actions at the time.

In those post-war years, the Anthroposophical Society passed through a critical period. As already briefly explained in chapter 1, up to the First World War, drawing out of its earlier association with the old Theosophical Society, the Society had been a comparatively small, closely knit fellowship of spiritual seekers. Membership then meant a steady and quiet study of esoteric science, in comparative seclusion and apart from the noisy issues of the day, under the close personal leadership of Rudolf Steiner. Those who look back on these early days spoke of them sometimes as of a lost paradise. They were the first witnesses of an event which occurs in the history of humanity only rarely and at very great intervals. The gates of the spirit world were opened, and there was a man, highly cultured but simple and unassuming, whose consciousness moved freely through these gates. His followers could sit at his feet at meetings which were yet small, they could put almost any question to him, they could visit him and consult him, they could ask him to be their personal guide and teacher.

All this began to change towards the end of the First World War, and changed radically after the war. Rudolf Steiner became a world figure, and the anthroposophical movement branched out into activities — educational, medical, agricultural, scientific — which involved it in the foundation of schools, clinics and other institutions, and which brought it cheek by jowl with an 'outside' world which was often anything but sympathetic. In particular the movement for the 'Threefold Social Order' which Steiner launched as his contribution to the reconstruction of Europe, and in which many thinking men and women have since recognized the foundations for the new world order towards which we must inevitably move, brought him and the anthroposophical movement embarrassingly close to the field of politics, and provoked the active hostility of many vested interests. It can be understood that a number of the older members of the Anthroposophical Society watched these developments with misgivings. Even some of the leaders wondered whether Rudolf Steiner was making a mistake and was, perhaps, sacrificing his esoteric mission for the sake of what to them were secondary activities.

The foundation of The Christian Community occurred when some of these tensions were at their height. In the circumstances it was not unnatural that the purpose of the Community could be misinterpreted. Although the Community was clearly meant to strike new ground and to develop independently as a religious body, the new movement, with its ritual and central spiritual purpose, appealed to some of the older members of the Anthroposophical Society as if it had been a resumption and continuation of Rudolf Steiner's own earlier esoteric activities. As a result of this in a number of towns the earliest meetings and services were crowded with members of the Anthroposophical Society, which made the approach for newcomers difficult if not impossible. In one or two places even the whole local anthroposophical group contemplated changing itself into a congregation of The Christian Community. We young people were too inexperienced to cope with this situation, and it must also be admitted that some priests were glad to have their services and meetings well attended without much effort on their part.

In this critical situation Rudolf Steiner came to the rescue. And in circumstances of this kind he did not mince his words. He recognized clearly the dangerous tendencies which might turn the Community and the Society into sectarian bodies. On December 30, 1922, during the last Christmas conference in the first Goetheanum, he devoted a whole evening to this problem of the right relationship between The Christian Community and the Anthroposophical Society. On this occasion he made a very earnest plea that anthroposophists should not simply submerge themselves in The Christian Community. Deeply anxious about the future of the Anthroposophical Society, whose energies, stability, sense of purpose and very economic security might be threatened by the powerful attraction of the new religious movement, he attempted to recall the members of the Anthroposophical Society to their first duty and loyalty by appealing almost to their pride, when he said that anthroposophists should have no need for religious renewal, and that The Christian Community should look after people who cannot take Anthroposophy but simply seek a modern form of the Christian religion. This was a hard saying, and he himself explained a few weeks later (in a lecture given in Stuttgart on January 25, 1923) that it was only his overwhelming anxiety (*allerschwerste Sorge*) for the safety and well-being of the Anthroposophical Society which had wrung these remarks from him. And he continued his explanation by saying: 'How could I possibly wish to criticize in any way whatever this movement for religious renewal? For it came into existence three and a half months ago out of what I myself advised, and it is the most natural thing that the prosperity of this movement should afford me the greatest satisfaction. I think that about this no doubt can exist whatsoever. But I felt compelled already after these three and a half

Hermann Poppelbaum on a visit to London in 1967 with Alfred Heidenreich.

months of [its] activity to speak those words in Dornach . . . And these words could not be anything but a paraphrase of this: Rejoice in the daughter, but don't forget the mother!'

Fortunately, these birthpangs and tensions, widespread as they were at the beginning, did not everywhere affect the young Christian Community in the same measure. For instance, in Frankfurt I was able to ask the members of the Anthroposophical Society to stay away for two years in order to give The Christian Community an independent start. This request was loyally complied with, and the relationship between the two sister movements soon became a very cordial one. We were indeed fortunate in having in Frankfurt an outstanding personality as leader of the local anthroposophical circles. He was Dr Hermann Poppelbaum who, after Rudolf Steiner and Albert Steffen, succeeded in 1964 as the third president of the General (international) Anthroposophical Society. During his years in Frankfurt, the Anthroposophical Society and The Christian Community, once it had been established, even shared the same premises in perfect harmony, the Anthroposophical Society having the use of them for three days a week, and The Christian Community for four days. Each group had its independent following, but our membership overlapped, which, given normal conditions, is a perfectly natural and healthy situation.

Steiner himself explicitly expressed the hope that the Community might carry the blessings of a balanced communal life into the broad fields of the anthroposophical movement. At the same time, he did not wish the anthroposophical movement to be dependent on this. In handling this problem, he made some profound revelations about the nature of communities and how they are formed. Communities as distinct from organizations contain an occult element. The members of a religious community share in an instintictive common reminiscence of their spiritual pre-existence. In particular, the communal experience of a true ritual wakens up in the worshippers those deeper levels of consciousness in which the memories of pre-existence are stored. At an anthroposophical meeting, he thought, community can be experienced by different means. He called it the 'waking up through meeting the soul and spirit of a fellow human being', which can be achieved 'when the content of Anthroposophy is experienced by a group of souls in an adequate manner'. And in rounding off the comparative similarities and differences of these parallel events he said, 'Speaking in pictures, one could put it that the sacramental community endeavours to call down the angels of the heavens into the place of worship so that they may be present among the human beings; the anthroposophical community endeavours to lift the human souls into the supersensory world so that they may come among the angels. This is the community-forming element in both bodies.'*

Many seeking souls have found and are finding that both ways of forming community are complementary and supplementary to each other. It can add to the richness of the spiritual life to share in both processes of experience. In Steiner's own words, 'That which must be clearly differentiated in the idea, is united again in the human being'.

However, the decision to become a member of The Christian Community, and the decision to become a member of the Anthroposophical Society should be two independent, clear and free decisions. The one does not, as a matter of course, involve the other. It is one of the constitutional principles of the Anthroposophical Society that one can become a member irrespective of one's religion, and that membership in the Anthroposophical Society does not imply that one need change either religion or church. 'The Anthroposophical Society should have room even for atheists', Rudolf Steiner said on occasion.

* Dornach, March 3, 1923.

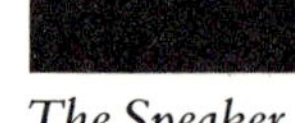

The Speaker.

In a characteristically informal mood.

Pictures of Alfred Heidenreich in the later years.

Approaching the summit of Great Gable, Lake District.

In conversation.

On the other hand, if an anthroposophist made up his mind consciously to join a church, then there was never any doubt that Rudolf Steiner thought it natural that he would join The Christian Community. Conversely, membership in The Christian Community does not necessarily involve membership in the Anthroposophical Society. There are people who will enthusiastically embrace the new Christian revelation without wishing to apply themselves to the study of occult science.

Apart from the right handling of questions of membership and organization the harmonious co-operation between The Christian Community and the Anthroposophical Society depends on the proper differentiation of function. For this Rudolf Steiner gave a simple guiding principle which belongs to the very foundation stones. 'The Anthroposophical Society', he said, 'addresses itself to man's need for knowledge and brings knowledge; The Christian Community addresses itself to man's need for resurrection and brings Christ.'* And it may be helpful to add a variation of the same principle expressed by Rudolf Steiner's successor as president of the General Anthroposophical Society, Albert Steffen, who formulated it like this, 'The anthroposophical movement addresses itself to those "in doubt", the Christian Community to those "in despair".' Naturally, the differentiation of function does again not imply a division of people. Very often, it is the same people who feel a need for knowledge *and* resurrection; and who at one time may be 'in doubt', at other times 'in despair'.

In practice it was not always so simple to follow these directions as it may seem to be in principle. But wherever they were followed, the work started on the right footing. In my own early field of activities it was a further fortunate circumstance that Dr Poppelbaum was a master of speaking to those in doubt, to those who above everything demanded knowledge. As a zoologist of standing whose scientific studies branched out more and more into other fields of biology, and who penetrated everything with the Goethean scientific vision as developed and enhanced by Rudolf Steiner, Dr Poppelbaum was an ideal exponent of spiritual *science.* He was able to lead his students right up to those fountain-heads of all living forms and beings, where Christ emerges as the Lord of Life, but he never indulged in the mistake, against which Rudolf Steiner had warned, of 'representing spiritual scientific endeavours as a substitute for the

* F. Rittelmeyer, *Rudolf Steiner Enters my Life*, p.140.

life and practice of religion'.* On The Christian Community side we did our best to learn to speak to those 'in despair', and to those 'seeking for resurrection'; but having had no experience or training for it and, in our youth lacking the natural maturity to do so instinctively, we did not find it easy. As we thus failed at times to speak with the authentic voice, we added to the confusion ourselves however unwittingly.

I have sometimes wondered to what degree Rudolf Steiner had reckoned with our immaturity and lack of competence. I have come to the conclusion that he knew it all. But, to use a homely phrase, the baby had to be born. The time was fulfilled for the new growing point to break out on the ancient tree of Christianity. And if we were only faithful and carried on with single purpose, the defects of our nature and our personal equipment would be mended. Perhaps the first fifty years had to be primarily a training ground for new priests, who would try to grow into the likeness of the supersensible pattern which Rudolf Steiner had revealed, without perhaps ever entering fully into the Promised Land themselves. But a new generation is rising who need not go through the same trials, the same lavish expenditure of try-outs, but who can start with a clearer concept, a firmer grasp on essentials, a steadier pace.

* Compare p.17.

7 Sacramental Communion and Cosmic Communion

Extra ecclesiam nulla salus, outside the Church there is no salvation — this is how the medieval Church formulated its crucial conviction. On this conviction it based its instruction and its policy. For the individual the visible test of being within this fold of salvation was to be 'a communicant member'. The sharing in the communion service showed whether a soul had taken its place within the process of salvation, or whether it was to be considered as lost.

The Church did not develop these views all at once. It took a very long time, in fact centuries, to complete the streamlining of its doctrine and discipline. Not until 1215 was the doctrine and policy concerning the communion service fully laid down, when, under the greatest of its ruling Popes, Innocent III, the medieval Church convened its most splendid Council. This, the famous Lateran Council, defined the doctrine of transubstantiation, decided to reserve the cup for the priests, made regular communion compulsory, and decreed auricular confession as an indispensable condition for admission to communion.

However, this iron discipline had not been inspired by truly Christian ideals, It was, in fact, a gigantic relapse into pre-Christian forms of organization. The totalitarian pattern of Egypt, Persia and other oriental theocracies had once more risen from the grave and descended on the communities of Christ. But the ghost of the Pharaohs could not survive for ever. Life advanced against death, the expanding consciousness of the

Gottfried Husemann (1900–72) was in charge of the training of priests from 1933 until his death. During this time he was also one of the three oberlenkers together with Alfred Heidenreich.

human individual strained at its chains, and the Reformers rose to overcome 'the Babylonian Captivity of the Church', as Luther put it in the title of one of his challenging pamphlets. Unfortunately, when the first wave of spiritual renewal had spent itself, and the reformed Churches were faced with the task of developing their own forms of order and discipline, the past began once more to assert itself. The Protestant churches became often as rigid as the medieval Church; and since they lacked its grandeur, their rigidity was not seldom petty and pathetic. They, too, asserted, or tried to assert, that there was no salvation outside the Church, but their conception of 'the Church' often shrank to the limits of their own particular brand.

Today all our ideas about 'the Church' must be recast. The time for monopolistic claims and monopolistic organizations is over. No single body can, in reality, be the sole possessor of the truth. Every honest attempt to observe the facts will make this clear. But there is no need for Christianity therefore to disintegrate into a number of warring sects. If we adjust our ideas, we can well conceive of a more living and organic 'unity' in which a great variety of 'diversities' can form a brotherly community.

The original seminary building in Stuttgart, erected in 1933, to house the training of priests. It was destroyed in the war and rebuilt in a similar style. This latter building is to be replaced by a much larger one in the 1980s, occupying the same and the adjacent site.

The distinctive contribution of The Christian Community to this process of rethinking can be most concisely illustrated by the sentence in which 'the Church' is referred to in the 'creed' which is said in the Act of Consecration of man. In the place of the traditional *credo in unam sanctam catholicam et apostolicam ecclesiam* (I believe in one holy Catholic and Apostolic Church), it states 'Communities whose members feel the Christ within them, may feel themselves united in a Church to which all men belong who are aware of the health-bringing power of the Christ'.

Whole centuries must have breathed a sigh of relief when this sentence was formulated. It proclaims the final release from Egypt and Babylon. If nothing else were left of Rudolf Steiner's work than his recasting of the Apostles' Creed, of which this sentence is part, it would establish his fame as a religious genius. Characteristically, in this rebirth of the creed, communities are taken as the basic units of the Church. The fact that the Christian Church consists of differentiated branches is taken as fundamental. The Book of Revelation comes to mind, which describes seven churches as typical patterns of Christian communities with their characteristic virtues and shortcomings. But the ideal Church in which individual 'Communities whose members feel the Christ within them may feel themselves united', is broad enough to embrace spiritually 'all men' as belonging to it 'who are aware of the health-bringing power of the Christ'. It has room for the solitary disciples, too, although it is somewhat unnatural and almost a contradiction in terms to be a Christian and not to be within the fellowship of a community.

(Whether the various 'Communities' which 'may feel themselves united' in this 'Church' form a World Council of Churches or some similar body on the level of physical organisation is another matter, and perhaps, then, of secondary importance. If such a Council is inspired by the organic idea of a free and living union of Communities, it can be a very important inter-denominational meeting place, and a means of speaking with an influential voice on world affairs. If, on the other hand, it sees itself as a pacemaker for a 'reunion' in terms of a universal, streamlined organization, it is in danger of serving the ghosts of the past.)

Nothing has greater power to form community than common worship. And sacramental worship in which time and again the same sacred procession of words, symbols and acts passes through the souls of those present, is the most uniting form of worship. In it also 'the health-bringing power of the Christ' is active in purest form.

In a true Eucharistic service the true selves of the worshippers are united with Christ. When we remember him, he remembers us, for he has promised to do so. But his memory is not tied to a mortal brain which allows only mere shadows of the past to arise. His 'memory' is a true 're-membering'. He is there where he sends his thoughts, he becomes a real 'member' of the congregation at the altar, and he can be in many places at the same time. When he told his disciples at the Last Supper, 'Do this in remembrance of me', he did not suggest a pale commemoration of a past event, but a re-living of his real presence in which he will truly co-operate. And while this union is enacted on the level of our selves, on another level those processes operate which have been described in chapter 3. Bread and wine carry Christ's healing forces into us in order to include even the body in the process of redemption, and to impress upon it, stage by stage, the incorruptible perfection of Christ's body of resurrection.

It is a profound tragedy that western scientific thought has cast the dark veil of agnosticism over the sacramental mysteries, and

Shalesbrook in Forest Row, Sussex, a centre in England for training priests, a course run in association with Emerson College.

that indifference and antipathy have become widespread, behind which often deeper perversities of human nature are hidden. Rudolf Steiner had something very pertinent to say about the inward opposition to sacramental ritual. 'I know', he said one day, 'how much antipathy to sacramental ritual lives in the hearts of modern people'. And he added that it is aroused by the same powers which in the Gospels say: 'We know thee, Jesus of Nazareth', and which begin to combat Christ because they recognize him.

Perhaps there are few things which penetrate so deeply to the core of the religious situation of today as this observation. The mental climate for the attitude which Rudolf Steiner characterized with such earnestness has been prepared, step by step, by the intellectual development of recent centuries, through which spirit and matter have been increasingly divorced from each other. It would indeed be a decisive victory for the demonic powers if they could finally inspire mankind with the belief that matter, or material energy, is really 'nothing but' matter, and has

Emil Bock (1895–1959) was the leader and spokesman of the younger group whose initiative led to the foundation of The Christian Community. He succeeded Rittelmeyer in 1938 as head of the Community. He was a formidable theologian, writer and speaker. Here on a visit to England in 1947 between Heidenreich and Husemann.

no place in the process of salvation. It would give the demons the eventual dominion over the earth because in the control of 'mere' matter they are supreme. Sacramental ritual in which matter is used for the sake of its intrinsic virtues, and thereby spiritualized, is the powerful and realistic antidote to the demonic aspirations.

However, almost alongside with the foundation of The Christian Community for which he mediated the communal sacramental mysteries in their modern Christian form, Rudolf Steiner spoke of ways and means by which the individual seeker for the spirit can for himself attain to union with the spiritual world. For this union Rudolf Steiner used the term 'cosmic communion'. This is a conception and a practice which played a part in Rudolf Steiner's life and a teaching from a comparatively early time. In the last quarter of the nineteenth century, when he was officially engaged in the editing of Goethe's scientific works, he published a series of books and studies in which he endeavoured to develop the philosophy and epistemology implied in Goethe's scientific method. In the course of these studies Rudolf Steiner formulated a sentence which seemed to him to express a vital element of Goethe's mental and spiritual activity. 'The perceiving of the Idea in the existing reality is the true communion of man.'

This sentence to which Rudolf Steiner frequently referred

back in later years, often in abridged or modified form, testifies to an experience, first observed in Goethe, which marks a historic stage in the evolution of human consciousness. The individual human soul has begun to be able freely and consciously to communicate with the objective world of the spirit, with the objective ideas which live in the things. And what in Goethe appeared as a seed, Rudolf Steiner developed to full flowering.

This fundamental step in the evolution of human consciousness was fully taken into consideration at the foundation of The Christian Community. It comes to expression in a characteristic quality which for all its vital significance is difficult to explain to outside enquirers. It is the fact that The Christian Community has no formulated body of doctrine, and that neither the members nor the priests are required to subscribe to any formula of faith. Characteristically the 'creed' referred to above does not contain the phrase 'I believe', but consists of a sequence of statements which if used in active contemplation leads eventually to a 'realization of the Idea in the existing reality' of created nature and history; in fact to a realization of the sacred Trinity of Father, Son, and Spirit.

There is, however, a still more intimate question to be answered. Is 'the perceiving of the Idea in the existing reality' all that is implied in 'cosmic communion', or is there more to it than that? In retrospect it appears as a great blessing that the more mature members among the founders were able, perhaps in anticipation of future problems, to put questions to Rudolf Steiner which solicited answers and directives which are of inestimable value, and which without such searching questions might never have been given. In *Rudolf Steiner Enters my Life* Friedrich Rittelmeyer relates how one day he asked Rudolf Steiner: 'Is it not possible to receive the body and blood of Christ without the bread and the wine, purely in meditation?' Rudolf Steiner answered: 'It is possible. From the back of the tongue it is exactly the same.' Here question and answer lead clearly beyond the first stage of 'the perceiving of the Idea in the existing reality'. They point to the ultimate fulfilment of the experience which was implied in Goethe's way of thinking. For is not the divine word which was incarnated in Christ *the* Idea in all perceived things? Here the communion of consciousness grows into a communion of being.

Perhaps the earnest and reverent seeker will ask one more question: 'Does transubstantiation, too, take place in this "cosmic" communion?' To this Rudolf Steiner answers in a lecture which he gave on December 31, 1922 in the first Goetheanum, only a few hours before the tragic destruction of that glorious building by fire. In this lecture to begin with he refers to Goethe's way of thinking, and says: 'Of these creative ideas I was able, in my small book *The Theory of Knowledge implicit in Goethe's World-Conception,* to say: this thinking represents the spiritual form of the communion of mankind.' Then he goes on to say that man will gradually be able to give of his own spiritual life to the world. 'Man changes it [the world] from out of his own spirit, if he gives of his own spiritual nature to the world, in that he raises his thoughts to Imagination, Inspiration, Intuition, in that he fulfils the spiritual communion of mankind.' And finally he gives the wonderful explanation, 'We should be conscious that, in our willing, in our willing permeated by love, we as human beings change back into spirit that which has become matter; that we perform a real transubstantiation, if we become conscious of our human place in the world, so that the activity of our thought and spirit grows really alive in us.'

These brief quotations give, of course, only the merest indication of what Rudolf Steiner outlined in that lecture as 'the beginning of a cosmic ritual appropriate for humanity at the present time'. And perhaps not very many people today would assert that they can as yet fully achieve what Rudolf Steiner has put before humanity as a task and as a possibility.

Nevertheless, these factors, too, are fully taken into consideration in the foundations of The Christian Community. From the beginning the conviction lived in the Community that the time is past when only he can be regarded as a full and true disciple of Christ and a member of his body who is a regular communicant at the altar. The Christian Community fully recognises the fact that the new age of Christianity which is beginning today includes a possible 'cosmic' communion for the individual.

Among the inner trends of the history of Christianity there has always been a tension between the 'sacramental' and the 'mystical' forms of the spiritual life. It was only natural that The Christian Community, as it evolved from its spiritual and historic background, should meet, too, with this deeply rooted

Rudolf Frieling (b. 1901) succeeded Bock in 1959. Before this he had worked for several years in the United States. He has written a number of important books, but it is as a religious speaker that he has made the greatest impression.

polarity in Christian life and practice. It was obviously those with the background of mysticism — the term used in its technical sense — who desired to probe more deeply into the field of individual 'cosmic' communion. And sometimes they went so far as to imagine a dividing line and even a mutually exclusive contrast between 'cosmic' and 'sacramental' communion. Once again, Rudolf Steiner's helping advice led the way to a true and balanced attitude. He pointed out that he, too, who in this manner received a kind of communion for his cognition (*Erkenntnis*) can most naturally receive communion also in another form. 'One should not emphasize the differences', he said, 'for of course the two ways do not contradict each other.'

One may well think that in this straightforward answer to a question Rudolf Steiner said only the obvious. But at the time, when we were all newcomers to the field of Christian renewal, his plain affirmation of the obvious was helpful and salutary. In a similar way, he dealt with the misguided notion that 'cosmic' Communion was thought to be 'superior' to 'sacramental' communion. 'This doubt', he said, 'which seems to have arisen that Anthroposophy is supposed to represent the sacrament as something of less importance or that something else should in the future take the place of the present movement — this dissension can only rest on an emotional misunderstanding.'

'Emotional misunderstandings' — *Gefühlsmissverständnisse* — who would wonder that they arose and at some moments threatened to cloud the clear vision of our path? But they were only birth-pangs which accompanied the revolutionary spiritual events. The surprising fact was not that they arose, but that in the end they impeded the foundation of the movement so little.

As time went on the true and organic relationship between sacramental and cosmic communion began to be worked out and is being worked out in the life and experience of many earnest seekers. Many of those who aspire to the experience of cosmic communion have testified to the help they have found in the Act of Consecration of Man, and in particular to the unfailing standard of sacramental reality which it provides. But also those for whom the Act of Consecration is the place of their normal communion know that in it they meet and receive Christ fully and in a manner entirely appropriate to the consciousness of the age.

In Rudolf Steiner's balanced guidance on this matter the spirit comes to full expression which had been active in Goethe whom, besides Rudolf Steiner, we venture sometimes to number among the 'fathers' of our Church. On the one hand Goethe had been the first in whom human consciousness had awakened to 'the spiritual communion of mankind' and who practised this communion in his creative life as artist and scientist. On the other hand, in his autobiography *Dichtung und Wahrheit*, Goethe testified to the central importance of sacramental communion in a passage which has been singularly neglected by his biographers and commentators.

> The sacraments are the highest part of religion, the visible symbols of divine grace. In the Lord's Supper earthly lips are allowed to receive the embodiment of a divine being, and partake of heavenly food in the form of earthly nourishment. Whether the sacrament is taken with more or less acceptance of the mystery, or with more or less accommodation to the intelligible, it always remains a great holy act, representative in the world of fact of what man can neither attain to nor do without. But such a sacrament

should not stand alone; no Christian can partake of it with the true joy for which it is given, if the symbolical or sacramental sense is not fostered within him. He must be accustomed to regard the inner religion of the heart and that of the external church as absolutely one, as the great universal sacrament, which again resolves itself into many others, and communicates to these separate rites its holiness, indestructibility and eternity.'

Goethe's sentences breathe at once an earnestness, insight and tolerance which strike us as prophetic. What he said was ahead of his time. It is our earnest hope and endeavour that his vision both of the sacramental life and of the Church may find a fulfilment in what we founded nearly half a century ago.

8 First Beginnings in the English-Speaking Countries

It will have been evident from the preceding chapters that from the beginning The Christian Community contained the seed of missionary expansion. At first, naturally, the message was carried to the countries where the German language is spoken: Germany, Austria and the German part of Switzerland. But like the ripples of a wave, before long the circle widened and the movement spread to the Scandinavian countries, the Netherlands and Czechoslovakia. These are countries which have indeed their own language and culture, but whose historical and cultural links with German-speaking Central Europe have for centuries been close, and where the majority of educated people could read a German book and follow a German lecture.

To carry The Christian Community into the English-speaking world was another matter. One would not be able to build on a similar cultural or religious groundwork. One would not be able to use the available Christian Community literature in German which was steadily growing. One would not be able to count on the regular co-operation of German-speaking priests and invite their visits, apart from very exceptional cases. One would have to begin in isolation and from nothing. Had it been indicated to choose the United States of America as the first stepping-stone into the English-speaking world, the opening would still have been easier. In choosing England the Community undertook its most difficult assignment up to date.

The insularity of English cultural life and in particular of

English religious life is proverbial. This insularity is all the more powerful since it is not only due to geographical reasons. Up to the fifteenth century England was very much part of Europe in spite of the twenty miles of water which separate it from the Continent. The isolation came about through historic events which are unique in modern history. Through the immortal deeds of Joan of Arc the bonds between England and the Continent were cut; and what appeared to Englishmen at the time as a humiliating defeat was in fact the making of England's special destiny. Rudolf Steiner spoke on repeated occasions of the part which Joan of Arc played. To him Joan's 'voices' were a spiritual fact which he investigated in his own way. He gave it as the result of these investigations that the Archangel Michael, acting as the servant of Christ, worked through 'the Maid', and was thereby directly instrumental in setting England free from continental entaglements, and in assigning to her 'an oceanic destiny'. Thus, in the circumstances which caused the relative isolation and insularity of England, one may clearly discern the finger of God.

It may not have been entirely by chance that it was in London, in May 1913, on the occasion of his last visit to the British Isles before the First World War, that Rudolf Steiner spoke for the first time, within the Anthroposophical Society, of the Archangel Michael as the inspiring guide of our present historic age. Perhaps this gesture was a hint that 'the Michael forces' were beginning to direct the destiny of England in a new manner.

This is, of course, not the place to discuss Rudolf Steiner's relationship to England in a general way, although it would make a fascinating study. But I can illustrate his views on the difficulties which would meet a spiritual pioneer movement which striving to serve the spirit of this age would begin its activities in England. Rudolf Steiner had first-hand experience. When the foundation meetings of The Christian Community started on September 6, 1922, he had only just returned from England. From August 16 to 29, he had been the chief lecturer at an educational conference at Oxford on 'Spiritual Values in Education and Social Life'. He was full of his impressions and began almost at once to speak of them. He gave some vivid pictures of Oxford and said how deeply serious and indeed inspiring he had found the spiritual life there. But he added a story which he said he couldn't help telling even his Oxford audience. 'If I had had to write a letter', he said, 'immediately after walking through the streets of Oxford and meeting scholars in their gowns, and if I had remained really true to myself, I should not have known if I should date my letter 750 BC or AD 1250. In no case would it have occurred to me to write the present date [1922]. It would simply not have been true to the situation.'

Both the depth and seriousness, but also the heavy and often unconscious traditionalism of English spiritual life was to meet us. In August 1924, in the last but one interview I was able to have with him, Rudolf Steiner himself took the initiative and began to speak about taking The Christian Community to England and America. As far as I am aware, he never brought the subject up on any other occasion. I remember the circumstances very vividly. Rudolf Steiner received his visitors in his studio. This was a kind of annexe to a large shed called *Schreinerei*, the carpenter's shop, in which much of the woodwork for the first Goetheanum was done. After the destruction of the Goetheanum on New Year's Eve 1922, a considerable part of this Schreinerei was enlarged and adapted as a make-shift lecture hall. But the centre part, from which doors led to the left into the hall, was still run as a carpenter's shop; and to the right a door led into the humble office and work-room of the master carpenter. In it the tall statue of Christ stood, not quite finished in its lower part, a telling symbol of the master's art. A small table was placed in the far corner with a few books lying open on it and a row of books at the back. At one end of the table and in a few other places bunches of red roses, their petals here and there falling to the ground, filled the room with a sweet smell of ripeness.

Rudolf Steiner received the visitor at the door, then he sat down in the middle of the room on a fragile-looking wicker chair. Another small table with an old-fashioned inkstand on it was just behind him, a little to the right. The visitor sat facing him. Everything in the room was of the utmost simplicity. Here Rudolf Steiner did most of his immense work; here he lay confined to bed for the last six months of his life; here he died.

The interview lasted about forty-five minutes. I was allowed to ask a number of questions concerning my personal life. When I had finished, Rudolf Steiner seemed to have still more time. So I ventured to change the subject and asked him whether he saw any prospects of our movement penetrating into Russia. He did not seem to take my question very seriously. He felt that perhaps it had not been asked with a very earnest purpose. He began to tell me stories of Rasputin, as if to indicate what type of man one would have to be in order to make a success in modern Russia. Then he changed his tone, in fact his whole attitude, almost abruptly and became deadly serious. He spoke of Central Europe. 'Germany will have the fate of Greece', he said. 'If you won't have, within three years, colonies in England and America, you will have nothing more to live on in Central Europe.'

These sentences for which I can recall every sound and intonation of Rudolf Steiner's voice, were a climax in the last few minutes of the interview. For some reason I buried them deeply in my mind. I believe I never mentioned them to anybody until long after I had settled in England. I certainly did not connect them with anything that I might have to do myself. Germany, Rudolf Steiner thought, would lose her political independence, she would cease to be 'a free country'. And situations would arise when free spiritual movements could only survive in Germany if assisted from England and America. Up till now this has hardly yet come about in a purely material sense. But when in the autumn of 1935 the Anthroposophical Society was prohibited in Germany by the Nazi authorities, help from England was decisive in saving The Christian Community from the same fate, then and for five more successive years. And no one can prophesy what the future holds.

'Within three years' Rudolf Steiner said, the Christian Community should be founded in England and America. In reality, it took three times three times three years before we opened our first centre in America, and five years before we made in 1929 a permanent begining in the British Isles.

One or two exploratory visits had been made by German priests prior to 1929. Emil Bock was in England in 1926 and in August 1928 Friedrich Rittelmeyer was invited to give two lectures at the first anthroposophical 'world conference' convened at Friends House, London. On this occasion I also came to London for the first time. I had taught myself to read English from a French grammar of English during my time as a prisoner of war. But I had never spoken a word of English before I set foot on English soil. So in preparation for the world conference I spent a four weeks' holiday in Southend-on-Sea — the cheapest place I could find from scanning advertisements — and began to

The first 'headquarters' was a room in Highgate, London, which served many purposes: as chapel, study, 'sitting room' and office.

train ear and tongue to English sounds by reading *The Times* leader every morning to my hostess. My hosts were Quakers, and in the generous time-honoured tradition of the Society of Friends, I was soon invited by various Quaker families for meals or treated to an open-air tea on the densely populated Southend beaches, where the density of occupation sometimes reached one body per square yard. Proceeding from Southend to the World Conference I met many interesting members of the English Anthroposophical Society, among them its General Secretary, Mr D. N. D. Dunlop. Mr Dunlop was an international figure by that time. His brain-child, 'the World Power Conference', through which the power-generating agencies, in particular the electricity companies, of Europe and overseas were linked, had made him known as a pioneer of economic co-operation instead of economic competition in the international field. He gave me a warm welcome and pledged his support to our plans.

On February 4, 1929 I pitched my tent in London for good, and from this date London has remained my legal domicile. Later in the year I was joined by Marta Heimeran who had been my fellow priest in Frankfurt and who in September 1929 became my wife. We settled in an attic in Highgate, and from the autumn of 1929 this became our headquarters. It consisted of one single

The first real home of The Christian Community in Britain — 1001 Finchley Road, London. In front the first car of the Community.

room which through transformation scenes reminiscent of a Christmas pantomime had to do as chapel, office, living room and bedroom, all in one. In the spring of 1931 we were able to acquire the house '1001 Finchley Road' which subsequently served us for over twenty years, and which with its fairy-tale number became something of an international celebrity. Unfortunately, at the time of this bold move the great economic depression had set in and the young Christian Community

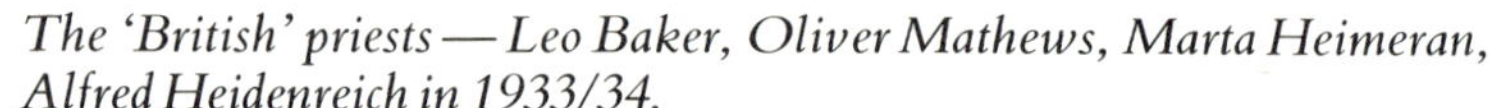

The 'British' priests — Leo Baker, Oliver Mathews, Marta Heimeran, Alfred Heidenreich in 1933/34.

Alfred Heidenreich and Marta Heimeran in the Garden 1933/34.

A group of the congregation with the Heidenreich family in the centre and Oliver Mathews in the back row, fourth from the right.

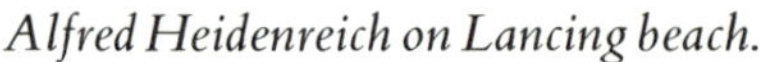
Alfred Heidenreich on Lancing beach.

Cecil Harwood, collaborator and advisor in the work of translating the Act of Consecration of Man into English.

passed through a severe test. There were times when the pennies were lacking for a loaf of bread, and we tasted what it is like to be kept awake at night by the nagging of physical hunger.

A very responsible and challenging task was the 'Englishing' of our rituals. An attempt had to be made, however imperfectly, to enter into the mysterious field where words have their origin in creative ideas and whence these ideas issue forth into the spoken form of a living language. In these endeavours we were most ably and helpfully assisted by Cecil Harwood, a profound English scholar who was for over thirty years the chairman of the Anthroposophical Society in Great Britain.

Tempting though it is to relate some of the strange, amusing and at times exasperating incidents of our early start in Britain, it is probably just as well to put the matter into one sentence and to say that, to start with, it was of course extreme uphill work and not at all easy to make contacts in a new and strange country. But I must offer a personal tribute of gratitude to Dr Sidney Berry, who was then the Secretary of the Congregational Union of England and Wales and later the first Secretary of the International Congregational Council. He invited me to speak at the 1929 May Meeting of the Congregational Assembly. It was my first public speech in English. The thunderous applause which followed was, of course, not due to my few halting sentences, but to the fact that at the time a determined attempt was made by the British Nonconformist Churches to break down the stony anti-German feeling which had survived from the First War. I was a sort of symbolic apparition in this setting. Ministers from Britain and overseas, and other delegates came up and shook me warmly by the hand and said 'No more war!' For many years until his death in 1961, Dr Berry remained a generous and ever ready friend whenever our Community needed help, and more than anybody else he opened for us doors to religious circles in England.

In June 1929, on Midsummer Day, the first Act of Consecration of Man was celebrated on British soil. It was in a small bungalow, belonging to Mr and Mrs R. Sargeant, at Lancing on the Sussex coast, where we had withdrawn to work undisturbed on the translation of our sacramental texts. A brief note which I wrote at the time into an exercise book for the record, reads:

The altar in the bedroom-cum-chapel.

The bungalow at Lancing on the Sussex coast where the Act of Consecration of Man was first held in English.

Croquet on the lawn. Alfred Heidenreich, Mrs & Mr Sargeant, Marta Heimeran.

Seven years ago the first group of men and women to start the *Christengemeinschaft* met about this time of the year at a little village by a lake in Bavaria in an old stable. Now we are going to bring our movement to another nation. Again the first group is together at a little village, but the lake has become a sea and the stable a bungalow. May this be a symbol of the growth and strength of our movement to be in this country.

July 5, 1929.

A brave venture to meet a post-war need, Albrighton Hall in Shropshire was purchased to provide a place where ex-servicemen could reorientate themselves towards a new future. For a time it became the administrative centre of the Community in Britain. After seven years needs had changed and it proved too costly to keep up. In 1953 conferences were moved to Woodford House, Keswick and the 'centre' returned to London.

The first big conference after the war attended by young people from the Continent.

An early post-war synod. Back: Stanley Drake, Donald Perkins, Adam Bittleston, Alfred Heidenreich, Oliver Mathews, Will Sawkins. Front: Eileen Hersey, Evelyn Francis [Capel], Marcia Dodwell.

In the summer of 1931 the first British-born priests were ordained. Oliver Mathews, our senior priest in Britain, dates his seniority from this event.

In the same year another event of some consequence occurred. One day a tall, bent, distinguished figure worked his way up the steep narrow steps which led to our attic at Highgate. He was the Revd John Arthur Bell, Secretary and Superintendent of the Homes for Little Boys at Farningham, Kent. These Homes, the first cottage orphanage in England, were a remarkable institution. Boys were received at kindergarten age, would go to school on the premises until school-leaving age, and would then be offered a full training in one of the trade departments which were part of the Homes. Tailors, shoemakers, carpenters, farmers would be trained, and — there was also a well-equipped printing shop. The Homes were not allowed to compete on the market, but in order to have practice material, they were free to print publications which would otherwise never be printed for lack of funds. Our publications qualified eminently under this rule, and so with the beginning of 1932 a printed *Christian Community Journal* began as a monthly magazine.

We had never dreamed that we could afford to have anything printed for years; but now we had a regular Journal, which

A British synod at Woodford House, Keswick in 1958. Standing: Peter Kändler, Oliver Mathews, Stanley Drake, Donald Perkins, Alfred Heidenreich, William Davie, Peter Roth, Adam Bittleston, Georg Klockner. Seated: Kalmia Bittleston, Marcia Dodwell, Eileen Hersey, Will Sawkins, Muriel Allen.

The church at Glenilla Road, London, has witnessed many important events, among them the ordination of Taco Bay and Peter Button in 1962. Here flanked by Alfred Heidenreich and Rudolf Frieling.

A British synod at Shalesbrook in 1978.

offered the chance of reprints as leaflets and booklets, and other exciting possibilities. It takes one's breath away if one thinks of the printing bills of those happy days. We had only to pay for paper and ink, so that a monthly issue of 1,000 cost normally not more than £2 2s. Naturally, as it was nearly all apprentice work, little problems and irregularities would occur. Two or three times a month, sometimes more often, I would sally down to Farningham in some slow train and talk things over. The able master printer, a formidable Scotsman, had to be kept sweet-tempered, and our Journal had to be steered towards a definite date through the competition of local parish magazines and the beautiful publications which the Homes did for themselves. But we got to know each other, and I learned a great deal of the mysteries of the black art, the orthodox ways of composition and layout, of the choice of paper, type and margin, of the 'tradition

1. Oliver Mathews; 2. Georg Klockner; 3. Adam Bittleston; 4. Friedrich Benesch (visiting); 5. Jon Madsen; 6. Peter Button; 7. Donald Perkins; 8. Michael Tapp; 9. Christopher West; 10. Kalmia Bittleston; 11. Roger Druitt; 12. Leonore Kovacs (visiting); 13. Peter Roth; 14. Ormond Edwards; 15. Rudolf Köhler; 16. Michael Jones; 17. Daniel Adcock; 18. Stanley Drake; 19. Muriel Allen; 20. Eric Sutton; 21. Helga Sudbrack; 22. Pearl Goodwin; 23. Eileen Hersey; 24. Evelyn Francis Capel; 25. Rachel Clayfield; 26. Louise Cais; 27. Irene Taylor; 28. Bill Boyd; 29. Baruch Urieli; 30. Elke Baublies; 31. Peter Allan. (William Davie was not present.)

of the House', and how to avoid the unforgivable sins of proof-reading.

The *Christian Community Journal*, thus happily started, has continued to appear regularly ever since 1932, although during the war years from 1941 to 1946 we had to fall back on duplication by mimeograph. The back numbers and bound volumes of this Journal contain some of our best writing in English and the most varied information of our movement.

The Journal has been of great help in building up a small publishing business, which like all our undertakings had to be started from nothing without any capital resources but with generous voluntary labour. Until 1976 it traded under the name of the Christian Community Press. Since then it has been known as Floris Books and has greatly extended its publishing programme.

At the time of the fiftieth anniversary in Britain the community had about thirty priests working there, not enough for the

Built in 1948 the church in Glenilla Road, London was a skilful adaption by Kenneth Bayes of a prefabricated factory design. The large trees have been felled since the picture was taken.

movement to work on a nationwide scale, but nevertheless with regular celebrations of the Act of Consecration of Man in over twenty places in widely dispersed geographical locations. For many years the only training college for the priesthood was in West Germany. More recently there has been a training programme in East Germany and in Britain.

The second decisive step within the English-speaking world, the move across the Atlantic, took a different form. Towards the end of the war I received letters from a — to me — unknown American gentleman in which he pleaded for the beginning of Christian Community activities in the United States and offered himself as a candidate for the priesthood. In those days all this seemed very far away. As I myself was cut off by war conditions from the other office-holders on the Continent who would have to have a say in the matter, I did not quite know what to do and, let it be confessed, never answered those letters. But Verner

Rudolf Koehler (b. 1899) started the work of the Community in Canada. He became an oberlenker in 1972.

Hegg — this was the name of the gentleman — persevered and as soon as the war was over, he appeared in England. His is the historic merit of having taken the first real initiative towards bringing The Christian Community permanently to the United States.

I say permanently, because already in 1928 a German priest, Wilhelm Hochweber, had been invited by American friends and had spent several months in the United States, especially in Chicago. During that time the Act of Consecration of Man was first celebrated on the American Continent (in German) and the first Christmas Midnight Service which Herr Hochweber celebrated in Brooklyn, New York, lives in the memory of friends who can recall it as a wonderful experience to which distance in time has lent additional enchantment.

In 1946, a British priest of the Community Adam Bittleston, together with Mr Hegg, went to the United States to test the situation afresh. Prospects and difficulties offered themselves in equal measure; but we had moved a considerable step nearer the goal. In December 1947 Mr Hegg was ordained in London, a

The first synod to be held in the United States, Chicago 1955, seven years after the first beginning. Verner Hegg, Rudolf Frieling, Rosemarie Bergmann, Rudolf Koehler (behind), Richard Lewis, Frederik Burgevin, John Hunter, Gregg Brewer.

An informal American group of priests in 1964. Gregg Brewer, Werner Grimm, Richard Lewis, John Hunter, Rudolf Koehler, Rosemarie Bergmann, Verner Hegg.

The house of The Christian Community in New York.

festival remembered by many as a historic occasion. Following this event, at last in the autumn of 1948 Mr Hegg and I made a determined bid to create a bridgehead in the United States. In two breathless months we roused the enthusiasm and won the support of a sufficient number of friends to make possible the purchase of a house as a first permanent home for the Community and its altar in New York. The dedication service on December 11, 1948 united a devoted gathering, and gave great joy in particular to members of The Christian Community who had emigrated to the United States as victims of Nazi oppression and who felt a sense of spiritual home again. They had supported our endeavours from the beginning. We enjoyed also the sympathetic and active backing of the leading members and in particular the warm blessing of the patriarch of the American Anthroposophical Society, Harry Monges, honorary president and for many years the foremost pioneer of Rudolf Steiner's work in the United States.

If one may venture a suggestion in these matters, I believe in those months Rudolf Steiner himself would have been pleased. Towards the end of his life he spoke frequently of the great catastrophes which he anticipated for the end of this century. And on occasion he seemed to imply that America and the

The first new church of the Community in America, at Devon, Pennsylvania, built in 1976.

North American synod at Copake, NY, in 1978. Standing: Diethart Jaehnig, Gisela Wielki, James Langbecker, John Hunter, Ita Bay (visiting), Gregg Brewer, Werner Grimm, Erk Ludwig, Rosemarie Bergmann, Hartmut Junge. Seated: Taco Bay (visiting), Richard Lewis, Robert Patterson, Phillip Nusbaum, Walter Brecker, James Hindes. (Verner Hegg and Carl Stegmann were not present.)

American people will hold a key position in these decisive and fearful events. Perhaps he took note of the fact and will know today that the heavenly light which the Christ had rekindled through him on his altars, has been lit on American soil among the American people. The springtide of Christianity has arrived in America too, and whatever the powers of darkness may achieve they will not prevail.

From these early beginnings the work in North America has grown and by 1978 there were sixteen priests serving eleven full-time centres (with a number of others served on a regular basis) in the states of California, Colorado, Illinois, Massachusetts, New York and Pennsylvania and in the provinces of Ontario and British Columbia. From 1961 North America had its own resident lenker* in Dr Rudolf Koehler who laid the foundations of the work in Canada. He was succeeded in 1972 by John Hunter.

In 1965 work was started in South Africa, first of all in the

A synod in South Africa in 1975. Julian Sleigh, Michael Heidenreich (the non-resident lenker, son of Alfred Heidenreich), Heinz Maurer, Neville Adams.

* *See* Foreword, p.8.

The Christian Community church in Johannesburg, built in 1975.

Cape and then four years later in Johannesburg.* In 1978 there were four priests working in the country with good prospects of an increase. Further afield, visits have been made to Australia and New Zealand. South America saw its beginnings in 1960 with centres in Brazil and Argentina.

* It was while on a journey to inaugurate this work in Johannesburg that Alfred Heidenreich died in 1969.

9 Growing Point

'Now the LORD said to Abram, "Go from your country and your kindred and your father's house to the land that I will show you."' These time-honoured words in their simple majesty present the archetypal pattern for the manner in which a new epoch opens in the spiritual evolution of humanity. In the last analysis, the origin and character of The Christian Community must be understood in reference to this pattern. At its outset there was a divine initiative and a human response or, to put it perhaps more correctly, a human groping, a muffled call, caused in the unconscious by divine readiness for a new step.

Every characteristic detail of the movement is as new as a new creation and at the same time as old as eterminty. This applies in a special sense to its centres of life: its sacramental events, seven in number, grouped around the Act of Consecration like the planets round the sun. And it remains now to be shown how they stand in relation to traditional forms.

The communion service, the Act of Consecration of Man, bears in its structure and sequence a distinct resemblance to the Mass. Yet not only is its language the vernacular of our age, but every single detail is as fresh and as new and as different as the fresh blossom of a new spring. Additions and accretions which were joined to the ritual body of the Mass in times of clouded vision have dropped away. The ritual has sprung again from its eternal source like a young reincarnation of its eternal self. It has gone through a metamorphosis caused by God himself.

Equally striking is the new birth of the ritual of baptism, the second great Christian sacrament. The baptismal service in The Christian Community is the first genuine form of infant baptism in the history of Christianity. All traditional forms of baptism used in the historic churches are more or less imperfect adaptations of a ritual originally used for adults. None of them meets the condition of a soul just entered into earthly life.

The traditional service of confirmation, hedged round and covered with doctrinal assumptions and demands of a bygone age, hardly gives to the adolescent boy and girl that true 'con-firmation', that is the strengthening of soul, which they need. The confirmation ritual in The Christian Community confers that grace and power which a Christianity can give which is in touch with the unseen reality of the world.

From the same sources the marriage ritual of the Community inspires a conception of marriage which adult men and women can accept and maintain with dignity and freedom. The burial services, too, which accompany and lead in reality the human self from one state of existence into the other witness to their more than human origin. And from the same sources also a form of sacramental consultation has come into being which can in time supersede the couch of the psvchoanalyst as much as the traditional confessional box.

These sacramental acts and events are the fountains of spiritual experience in The Christian Community. They help us to make the whole of life into a sacrament in reality. Without the constant inspiration of the 'special' sacraments the 'universal' sacrament of life remains mostly a pious ideal. Anyone who in his own judgment and conviction has come to realize the truth of our sacraments can become a member. No other condition is required. One ultimate gift and gain of these sources of sacramental experience is of crucial importance for all religion. They lead to a fresh first-hand realization of man's immortal self. We have no quarrel with science, when science asserts that consciousness as we know it in our ordinary, everyday, waking state of mind, is tied to the brain, to the cerebro-spinal system, is 'cell-bound'. But we know from the sources of experience opened up by the sacramental events that within us there is an occult entity, the 'real I'. It may be that in the past — or at any rate in the last few centuries — this real I could never be convincingly experienced this side of death by the majority of men and women. But this situation is changing. And in the process we cease to 'worry' about our immortality or to make any fuss about it. Our 'immortality' begins to dawn within our consciousness; it emerges as a knowable fact: it explains that 'dormant omniscience' in us, of which some writers speak. Together with this knowable realization of our eternal entity we discover not only that we shall continue to have an individual existence after death, however much our type of consciousness may be changed, but that in fact we had an individual existence before physical conception and birth.

With this first-hand discovery (or rediscovery?) of our eternal self, our whole approach to the other fundamentals of religion undergoes a change. Our vision of God, or as today we incline to say more naturally, of 'the divine world of spirit', our grasp of the incarnation, death and resurrection of Jesus Christ and their redemptive significance takes on a new life, our practice of prayer and meditation, our approach to the whole range of practical morality — everything changes or rather is reborn and refashioned.

In the sharing of these experiences and the gradual working out of an image of man, the universe and God based on these sources of experience, the Community finds its unifying force. It is obvious that in this process the teaching of Rudolf Steiner, who penetrated in his own way into the unseen world where our real I has its being, is of inestimable value. But neither Steiner's nor anyone else's teaching past or present plays the part of 'doctrine' in The Christian Community. Strictly speaking, there is no doctrine. In fact, priests and members alike are constitutionally assured of complete freedom not only of conscience, but also of thought and belief. Such authority as is necessary for the co-ordinated conduct of a religious movement is only concerned with the distribution of human forces, the ordering of public activities, and the administration of physical needs.

The Movement, it is true, has a creed which is normally spoken by the priest in the communion service. But as already pointed out it does not contain the phrase 'I believe'. It is an instrument of meditation which the individual seeker may or may not wish to use for his personal contemplation. It offers the fundamental facts of Christianity in twelve simple sentences which may draw a free response from a seeking mind.

From these sources of experience we draw the faith by which

we try to live. Faith with us *follows*, not precedes, knowledge. Faith with us is not a belief in things unknown and unknowable, or an acceptance on authority of a body of revealed teaching, but a state of active concern, almost a state of universal love engendered by the voyage of discovery into the fields of supersensible truth.

It is understandable that a religious movement with this unusual character and qualities presents a puzzle to other religious bodies. We cannot pretend that our advent was universally welcomed by organized Christianity. The traditional bodies did not quite know what to make of us. In Central Europe the Community has been called a '*kirchenähnliches Gebilde*', a 'church-like something'. This is not a bad description. In one way, for all practical purposes we are a church. We hold services, christen babies, confirm young people, celebrate marriages, and conduct funerals. We give religious instruction to children, provide Bible classes and group-studies on other religious subjects, and offer our services of pastoral care. From all this we might be regarded as a denomination. On the other hand we attach no claim to our services, not only in the narrow economic sense that we do not charge 'fees' for our ministrations, but also in the wider sense that we offer our services to members and non-members alike; in fact to anyone who sincerely desires them. On these grounds we might be regarded as an inter-denominational movement.

The fact is, we do not easily fit into an existing category on any level. But I suppose this is the nature of a growing point. It breaks free of accepted patterns and follows its own laws of growth and form.

Of course, as time went on, other religious bodies expressed their opinion more definitely, friendly and unfriendly, but generally puzzled and not seldom a little scared. The first General Secretary of the World Council of Churches, W. A. Visser 't Hooft, wrote a small book on what he calls 'the choice between syncretism and Christian universalism', with the title *No Other Name*. The book is a kind of farewell message on the occasion of his retirement after thirty years' ecumenical service, and is as authoritative a survey of Christian movements today as a condensed, concentrated presentation will allow. Visser 't Hooft writes about The Christian Community from a neutral but not unfriendly point of view. He pays tribute to our theology which 'has impressive features in that it seeks to arrive at an interpretation of the total cosmic process' and refers to our Christology which 'seeks to bring together the historic Jesus and the cosmic Christ'. But he says that with us 'the story of the great deeds of God is transformed into a record of cosmic processes through which, exactly as in the old gnostic systems, the spiritual core of man is progressively released from earthly bondage. . . . The gospel is forced into a framework which is foreign to it.'

This statement is fairly representative of the general view which organized Christianity has formed up to date about our movement. It is characteristic in that it looks for the theology, the 'doctrine' of our Community, as the distinctive feature, but fails to observe the life. This is an inevitable pitfall for the traditional approach which believes that one can get to know a growing point from books. With this approach of viewing our Community as it were from outside, it is very tempting to look for a label culled from history, which may seem to fit the case. By fastening this label to the phenomenon, one thinks one can pigeon-hole it — and forget about it. It has been 'attended to'. 'Gnostic' is a very handy label in our case. But it begs the question. For one solid result of our so-called Gnosticism is the clear discovery and recognition of the true Incarnation, Death and Resurrection of Christ — which in one form or other all gnostic systems denied.

What our 'separated brethren' really mean, when they call us gnostics, is our assertion that a modern Christian can have first-hand access to the unseen world. Of this they are very naturally apprehensive. For it is dynamite for all established positions.

Realizing this difficulty we cannot help feeling somewhat uncomfortable in the fellowship of other churches, although we approach them with every good will. It has made us hesitate so far to become a member of the World Council of Churches, although we have shared in ecumenical meetings and conversations with benefit, we hope, for both sides. We are entirely open and willing to share our discoveries, and we have no intention to use them for making proselytes. We feel that our mission is to the countless souls who have turned their back on organized Christianity, either from indifference or disappointment, and we believe we have the spiritual nourishment for which they hunger. If other religious bodies wish to benefit from our experience, they are welcome to it.

In this context I cannot ignore another stumbling-block. It will have become apparent from earlier parts of this story that The Christian Community has a professional ministry with its own orders. Together with the other sacramental acts referred to above, the ritual of ordination, of consecrating priests, has also been reborn. For those churches which believe in the Apostolic succession this is an impossible challenge. All the more so because our movement does not claim what is usually called 'a special revelation', vouchsafed perhaps for a special purpose, but feels that it treasures a universal renewal of the Christian order of priesthood. This is, in fact, the very core of the growing point. On this core all the rest depends. For it is not possible to perform a valid sacramental act without the spiritual enablement conferred by valid orders.

We have never thought it necessary to argue out in theory what consequences follow from the fact that a new Christian succession has been founded. Of its reality we have never had a shadow of doubt.

In this most central precinct of our movement the relationship to universal Christianity becomes still clearer. Our roots in Christ are vertical, not horizontal. We have no direct link with the historic bodies. Adapting a famous phrase of Ralph Waldo Emerson, we are not a church of memory, but the church of hope.

We believe we have reason to know that the living Christ is making a new approach to the human race in order to help it step forward from natural evolution to spiritual evolution. Naturally, the powers of evil and hindrance do everything to oppose and obscure this new advent. Much of this is foretold in the eschatological chapters of the Gospel, where Christ speaks of 'the last things'. It is true that some Christian scholars think that these chapters are also part of 'a frame-work which is foreign' to what they think is 'the Gospel'. But if these chapters are taken as *an archetypal pattern for apocalyptic times,* they hand us a key for the understanding of our age in Christ's own words, and with it we can comprehend the significance of a fresh *Christian growing point.*

Subject and Name Index

References in *italics* are to illustrations

Chronological Index

to the events mentioned in the book

References in *italics* are to illustrations

Acknowledgements

N. Adams 116; T. Bay 30; A. Cais 113, 114; M. Heidenreich 8, 12, 14, 25, 29, 38, 39, 42, 45, 48, 60, 71, 74, 78, 80, 84, 85, 87, 88, 91, 99, 100, 101, 102, 103, 104, 105, 106, 107, 110, 111, 112, 115; R. Patterson 114; Philosophisch-Anthroposophischer Verlag 58; F. Rauter 102; M. Tapp 57, 108; Verlag Urachhaus 25; Frau Wagner 25, 38, 39, 40. While every effort has been made to trace the original author of the photographs this has not always been possible.